TREASURY OF HELPFUL VERSE

HOPE.

From the painting by Anton Dvorak.

A Treasury of Helpful Verse

Selected by
John White Chadwick
and
Annie Hathaway Chadwick

Illustrated

Granger Index Reprint Series

BOOKS FOR LIBRARIES PRESS
FREEPORT, NEW YORK

First Published 1896
Reprinted 1969

STANDARD BOOK NUMBER:
8369-6007-6

LIBRARY OF CONGRESS CATALOG CARD NUMBER:
73-76933

DEDICATION.

Good courage!   Yea, my father, thou hast had
   Thy part in this on many a stormy sea,
   When the great winds were blowing mightily
And all the waste of waters had gone mad
And struck at heaven; and when — most drear and
      sad
   Of all remembered things! — the empyry
   Smiled as if glad that such wide wreck could be,
While strong men's hearts could not be comforted.
Now thou hast gone upon a voyage far
   Beyond the sea-mark of thy venturous prime,
Steering thy course by a remoter star
   Than the remotest which our heavens climb:
Will thy heart sink, thy courage fail thee?   No;
Fearless as ever thou dost onward go.

J. W. C.

NOTE.

THE sub-title of our book, "Songs of Good Courage," must not be too rigidly interpreted. It represents, we trust, its dominant tone, but the courage we have sought to illustrate is of many kinds: the courage of belief is here, and also the courage of doubt; the courage of rejoicing faith, and the courage to live grandly and do well however that may be denied. We have sought, too, the things that make for courage, and those, as well, that make for comfort and for peace. There are others which respect the rights of sorrow and give voice to aching hearts. We have trenched as little as possible on other anthologies with which we are acquainted, and upon the familiar classics, but occasionally have pounced upon our own wherever we have found it, being unable to deny ourselves some things which we have loved together many years. When poems have been taken entire we have followed the authors' titles, but many of our pieces are fragments, and for these we have invented titles which we trust the authors will not disapprove.

Our book could not have been made without the kind assistance of many authors and publishers who have allowed us the use of their poems and their publications. To the Century Company we are particularly obliged for the poems of R. W. Gilder and James

Whitcomb Riley; to Harper and Brothers for the three poems taken from Mr. Howells's "Stops of Various Quills;" to Charles Scribner's Sons for the selections from Sidney Lanier; and to Houghton, Mifflin and Company for a wide range of pieces from our major poets and from Miss Cone, Miss Guiney, Mr. William Roscoe Thayer and others, later born. To Mr. Gilder we are particularly indebted for his permission to use the initial phrase of the first poem as the title of our book.

BROOKLYN, May 17, 1896.

INDEX OF AUTHORS.

———◆———

LIST OF ILLUSTRATIONS

———◆———

TREASURY OF HELPFUL VERSE.

THROUGH LOVE TO LIGHT.

THROUGH love to light! Oh, wonderful the way
　　That leads from darkness to the perfect day!
From darkness and from sorrow of the night
To morning that comes singing o'er the sea.
Through love to light! Through light, O God, to thee,
　　Who art the love of love, the eternal light of
　　　　light.

RICHARD WATSON GILDER.

THE BETTER WAY.

'TIS sweet to hear of heroes dead,
　　To know them still alive;
But sweeter if we earn their bread,
　　And in us they survive.
Our lives should feed the springs of fame
　　With a perennial wave,
As ocean feeds the babbling founts
　　Which find in it their grave.

HENRY D. THOREAU.

WHEN DUTY CALLS.

IN an age of fops and toys,
  Wanting wisdom, void of right,
Who shall nerve heroic boys
  To hazard all in Freedom's fight, —
Break sharply off their jolly games,
  Forsake their comrades gay,
And quit proud homes and youthful dames
  For famine, toil, and fray?
Yet on the nimble air benign
  Speed nimbler messages,
That waft the breath of grace divine
  To hearts in sloth and ease.
So nigh is grandeur to our dust,
  So near is God to man,
When Duty whispers low, *Thou must*,
  The youth replies, *I can*.

                              RALPH WALDO EMERSON.

THREE FRIENDS.

HATH he not always treasures, always friends,
  The good great man? — three treasures, love
      and light,
And calm thoughts, regular as an infant's breath;
And three firm friends, more sure than day and
      night, —
Himself, his Maker, and the angel Death.

                              SAMUEL TAYLOR COLERIDGE.

THE BIRD OF LIFE.

L ET us be like a bird, a moment lighted
  Upon a twig that swings;
He feels it sway, but sings on unaffrighted,
 Knowing he hath his wings.
       VICTOR HUGO.

MULTUM IN PARVO.

I T is not growing, like a tree,
  In bulk, doth make man better be;
Or standing long an oak, three hundred year,
To fall a log at last, dry, bald, and sere:
   A lily of a day
   Is fairer far in May,
 Although it fall and die that night, —
 It was the plant and flower of Light.
In small proportions we just beauties see;
And in short measures life may perfect be.
       BEN JONSON.

THE WAY TO GLORY.

Y EA, let all good things await
  Him who cares not to be great
But as he saves or serves the state.
Not once or twice, in our rough island-story,
The path of Duty was the way to glory:
He that walks it, only thirsting
For the right, and learns to deaden

Love of self, before his journey closes
He shall find the stubborn thistle bursting
Into glossy purples, which outredden
All voluptuous garden-roses.
Not once or twice, in our fair island-story,
The path of Duty was the way to glory:
He that, ever following her commands,
On with toil of heart and knees and hands,
Through the long gorge to the far light has won
His path upward, and prevailed,
Shall find the toppling crags of Duty scaled
Are close upon the shining table-lands
To which our God himself is moon and sun.

ALFRED TENNYSON.

A TRUE PATRIOT.

I LOVED my country so as only they
    Who love a mother fit to die for may;
I loved her old renown, her stainless fame,—
What better proof than that I loathed her shame?

JAMES RUSSELL LOWELL.

GOD WITH US.

O POWER more near my life than life itself,
    I fear not thy withdrawal: more I fear
Seeing to know thee not, hoodwinked with dreams
Of signs and wonders, while, unnoticed, thou,
Walking thy garden still, commun'st with men,
Missed in the commonplace of miracle.

JAMES RUSSELL LOWELL.

PURITANS GOING TO CHURCH.

From the painting by G. H. Boughton.

COR CORDIUM.

OUR God is never so far off
    As even to be near.
He is within; our spirit is
    The home he holds most dear.
To think of him as by our side
    Is almost as untrue
As to remove his throne beyond
    Those skies of starry blue.
So all the while I thought myself
    Homeless, forlorn, and weary,
Missing my joy, I walked the earth,
    Myself God's sanctuary.

FREDERICK W. FABER.

MATER TRIUMPHALIS.

MOTHER of man's time-travelling generations,
    Breath of his nostrils, heartblood of his heart,
God above all gods worshipped of all nations,
    Light above light, law beyond law thou art.

Thine hands, without election or exemption,
    Feed all men fainting from false peace or strife,
O thou, the resurrection and redemption,
    The godhead and the manhood and the life.

ALGERNON C. SWINBURNE.

STRONG–BUILDED WORLD.

STRONG–BUILDED world of ancient days,
   Shown to me for a dwelling-place,
With heights and depths, and many a treasure, —
Come, I will count, and weigh, and measure,
And know you, house in which I live!
And what your chambers have to give;
And far more sure and far more swift
Shall be my use of every gift;
From land to land, from age to age,
Larger shall grow my heritage.

And you, great over-bending roof!
You rolling lights that shine aloof
Forever, I will know you too,
And why you shine, and what you do;
And when I know your paths and ways,
That, too, shall help me through the days,
Across the seas, and round the land,
As if God led me by the hand.

He leadeth me, he makes me care
For every pain his creatures bear!
I will arise and ask aloud
Of every pain that cries to God,
How it has come.   And I shall know,
I shall, I shall, — God tells me so.
And many a pain shall pass away
Like darkness in the light of day.

Amen! Thus spake the soul of man
In every age since time began;
And louder yet and clearer grows
That voice divine since first it rose:—
"Wisdom and Love, not Wrath and Chance,
Showed me this fair inheritance;
And till I know it as I ought,
I know not all they meant and thought
When first they showed my world to me,
Nor all that I was meant to be."
Thou gracious voice! go sounding on
Till all the inheritance be won.

WILLIAM BRIGHTY RANDS.

THE CLOUD OF WITNESSES.

LIVING, our loved ones make us what they dream;
Dead, if they see, they know us as we are.
Henceforward we must be, not merely seem;
Bitterer woe than death it were by far
To fail their hopes whose love can still redeem;
Loss were thrice loss which thus their faith could mar.

ARLO BATES.

CIVITAS DEI.

THERE is a city, builded by no hand,
And unapproachable by sea or shore,
And unassailable by any band
Of storming soldiery for evermore.

T. W. PARSONS.

VICTORIOUS.

STAINLESS soldier on the walls,
    Knowing this — and knows no more:
Whoever fights, whoever falls,
    Justice conquers evermore;
And he who battles on her side,
    God, though he were ten times slain,
Crowns him victor glorified, —
    Victor over death and pain
        Forever.
                        RALPH WALDO EMERSON.

LOVE INESCAPABLE.

THERE 'S nothing in the world, I know,
    That can escape from love;
For every depth it goes below,
    And every height above.
It waits, as waits the sky
    Until the clouds go by,
Secure when they are gone
    And when they stay.
                        HENRY D. THOREAU.

DAYS.

DAUGHTERS of Time, the hypocritic Days,
    Muffled and dumb like barefoot dervishes,
And marching single in an endless file,
Bring diadems and fagots in their hands.

To each they offer gifts after his will, —
Bread, kingdoms, stars, and sky that holds them all.
I, in my pleachèd garden, watched the pomp,
Forgot my morning wishes, hastily
Took a few herbs and apples, and the Day
Turned and departed silent.   I, too late,
Under her solemn fillet saw the scorn.

RALPH WALDO EMERSON.

THE UNENDING GENESIS.

I THINK man's soul dwells nearer to the east,
Nearer to morning's fountains than the sun, —
Herself the source whence all tradition sprang,
Herself at once both labyrinth and clew.
The miracle fades out of history,
But faith and wonder and the primal earth
Are born into the world with every child.

JAMES RUSSELL LOWELL.

LIKE IN DIFFERENCE.

DOUBTING Thomas and loving John,
With the others walking on.

" Tell me now, John, dare you be
One of the small minority;
To be lonely in your thought,
Never to be sought or bought;

To be dropped and shunned, and go
Through the world esteemed its foe;
To bear off your titles well,
Heretic and infidel;
To be singled out and hissed,
Pointed at as one unblessed;
Warred against in whispers faint,
Lest the children catch a taint?
If you dare, come now with me,
Fearless, confident, and free."

" Thomas, do you dare to be
One of the great majority;
To be only as the rest,
With God's common blessings blest;
To accept in humble part
Truth that shines on every heart;
To be never set on high
Where the envious curses fly;
Never name and fame to find,
Far outstripped in soul or mind;
To be hid, except to God,
As one grass-blade in the sod,
Under foot with millions trod?
If you dare, come, with us be
Lost in love's great unity."

EDWARD ROWLAND SILL.

WILL.

OH, well for him whose will is strong!
    He suffers, but he will not suffer long;
He suffers, but he cannot suffer wrong.
For him nor moves the loud world's random mock,
Nor all Calamity's hugest waves confound;
Who seems a promontory of rock,
That, compassed round with turbulent sound,
In middle ocean meets the surging shock,
Tempest-buffeted, citadel-crowned.

But ill for him who, bettering not with time,
Corrupts the strength of heaven-descended will,
And ever weaker grows through acted crime,
Or seeming-genial venial fault,
Recurring and suggesting still!
He seems as one whose footsteps halt,
Toiling in immeasurable sand,
And o'er a weary, sultry land,
Far, beneath a blazing vault,
Sown in a wrinkle of the monstrous hill,
The city sparkles like a grain of salt.

ALFRED TENNYSON.

THE SAFEST WAY.

THOUGH love repine and reason chafe,
    There came a voice without reply,
'T is man's perdition to be safe
    When for the truth he ought to die.

RALPH WALDO EMERSON.

EVENING PRAYER.

ERE on my bed my limbs I lay,
   It hath not been my use to pray
With folded hands or bended knees;
But silently, by slow degrees,
My spirit I to love compose,
In humble trust mine eyelids close
With reverential resignation:
No wish conceived, no thought expressed,
Only a sense of supplication, —
A sense o'er all my soul imprest
That I am weak but not unblest,
Since in me, round me, everywhere,
Eternal Strength and Wisdom are.

SAMUEL TAYLOR COLERIDGE.

IN A RING.

GOD wills that in a ring
   His blessings should be sent
From living thing to thing,
   And nowhere stayed or spent;
And every soul that takes
   And gives not on again
Is so a link that breaks
   In heaven's love-made chain.

WILLIAM BARNES.

EVENING PRAYER.

From the painting by Meyer von Bremen.

UNRECOGNIZED.

WHEN we have gone within the veil that hides
        From mortal ken the lost of other days,
    Amid the pure transparence of those rays
Wherein, unseen, the Light of Life abides,
Shall we indeed from out the luminous tides
        Of spirits surging through those mystic ways
        Full surely know — oh, joy beyond all praise ! —
Each waiting friend?   So heart to heart confides
Its secret pain.   But one of clearest sight,
        So questioned, answered : While we still are here
        Earth-pent, how often do we recognize,
For what they are, the spirits pure and bright
        Close at our sides?   How not for heaven fear
        When mortal vapors wrap in such disguise ?

JOHN WHITE CHADWICK.

GREATER THAN WE KNOW.

WE men who in the morn of youth defied
        The elements must vanish ; be it so !
Enough if something from our hands have power
To live, to act, and serve the future hour ;
And if, as toward the silent tomb we go,
Through love, through hope, and faith's transcendent
            dower,
We feel that we are greater than we know.

WILLIAM WORDSWORTH.

AFTER MANY DAYS.

NOT out of any cloud or sky
        Will thy good come to prayer or cry.
Let the great forces, wise of old,
Have their whole way with thee,
Crumble thy heart from its hold,
Drown thy life in the sea.
And æons hence, some day,
The love thou gavest a child,
The dream in a midnight wild,
The word thou would'st not say, —
Or in a whisper no one dared to hear, —
Shall gladden earth and bring the golden year.

        EDWARD ROWLAND SILL.

A MARCHING SONG.

WITH us the fields and rivers,
        The grass that summer thrills,
The haze where morning quivers,
        The peace at heart of hills,
The sense that kindles nature, and the soul that fills.

With us all natural sights,
        All notes of natural scale;
With us the starry lights;
        With us the nightingale;
With us the heart and secret of the worldly tale, —

The strife of things and beauty,
    The fire and light adored,
Truth and life-lightening duty,
    Love without crown or sword,
That by his might and godhead makes man god and
        lord.

These have we, these are ours,
    That no priests give nor kings;
The honey of all these flowers,
    The heart of all these springs;
Ours, for where freedom lives not, there live no good
        things.

Rise, ere the dawn be risen;
    Come, and be all souls fed;
From field and street and prison
    Come, for the feast is spread;
Live, for the truth is living; wake, for the night is dead.

                                ALGERNON C. SWINBURNE.

THE GREATEST GIFT.

NO good is certain but the steadfast mind,
        The undivided will to seek the good:
'T is that compels the elements, and wrings
A human music from the indifferent air.
The greatest gift a hero leaves his race
Is to have been a hero.

                                GEORGE ELIOT.

THE MODERN RHYMER.

NOW, you who rhyme, and I who rhyme,
    Have we not sworn it, many a time,
That we no more our verse would scrawl,
For Shakespeare he had sung it all;
And yet, whatever others see,
The earth is fresh to you and me;
And birds that sing, and winds that blow,
And blooms that make the country glow,
And lusty swains, and maidens bright,
And clouds by day, and stars by night,
And all the pictures in the skies
That moved before Will Shakespeare's eyes;
Love, hate, and scorn; frost, fire, and flower; —
On us as well as him have power.
Go to! our spirits shall not be laid,
Silenced and smothered by a shade.
Avon is not the only stream
Can make a poet sing and dream;
Nor are those castles, queens, and kings
The height of sublunary things.

Beneath the false moon's pallid glare,
By the cool fountain in the square
(This gray-green, dusty square they set
Where two gigantic highways met)
We hear a music rare and new,
Sweet Shakespeare, was not known to you!
You saw the new world's sun arise;
High up it shines in our own skies.

You saw the ocean from the shore, —
Through mid-seas now our ship doth roar;
A wild, new, teeming world of men
That wakens in the poet's brain
Thoughts that were never thought before
Of hope, and longing, and despair,
Wherein man's never-resting race
Westward, still westward, on doth fare,
Doth still subdue and still aspire,
Or, turning on itself, doth face
Its own indomitable fire: —
O million-centuried thoughts that make
The Past seem but a shallop's wake!

RICHARD WATSON GILDER.

AUTOCHTHON.

I AM the spirit astir
    To swell the grain,
When fruitful suns confer
    With laboring rain;
I am the life that thrills
    In branch and bloom;
I am the patience of abiding hills,
    The promise masked in doom.

When the sombre lands are wrung,
    And storms are out,
And giant woods give tongue,
    I am the shout;

2

And when the earth would sleep,
   Wrapped in her snows,
I am the infinite gleam of eyes that keep
   The post of her repose.

I am the hush of calm;
   I am the speed,
The flood-tide's triumphing psalm,
   The marsh-pool's heed;
I work in the rocking roar
   Where cataracts fall;
I flash in the prismy fire that dances o'er
   The dew's ephemeral ball.

I am the voice of wind
   And wave and tree,
Of stern desires and blind,
   Of strength to be;
I am the cry by night
   At point of dawn,
The summoning bugle from the unseen height,
   In cloud and doubt withdrawn.

I am the strife that shapes
   The stature of man,
The pang no hero escapes,
   The blessing, the ban;
I am the hammer that moulds
   The iron of our race,
The omen of God in our blood that a people behold,
   The foreknowledge veiled in our face.

            CHARLES G D. ROBERTS.

HOPE.

From the painting by Burne-Jones.

"WHY THIS WASTE?"

THAT eyes which pierced our inmost being through;
   That lips which pressed into a single kiss
  It seemed a whole eternity of bliss;
That cheeks which mantled with love's rosy hue;
That feet which wanted nothing else to do
   But run upon love's errands, this and this;
   That hands so fair they had not seemed amiss
Reached down by angels through the deeps of blue, —
   That all of these so deep in earth should lie
   While season after season passeth by;
That things which are so sacred and so sweet
The hungry roots of tree and plant should eat!
   Oh for one hour to see as thou dost see,
   My God, how great the recompense must be!

JOHN WHITE CHADWICK.

A GOOD HOPE.

MY own hope is a sun will pierce
   The thickest cloud earth ever stretched;
That after last returns the first,
  Though a wide compass round be fetched;
That what began best can't end worst,
  Nor what God blest once prove accurst.

ROBERT BROWNING.

SLEEP.

WHEN to soft Sleep we give ourselves away,
    And in a dream as in a fairy bark
Drift on and on through the enchanted dark
To purple daybreak, little thought we pay
To that sweet-bitter world we know by day.
We are clean quit of it, as is a lark
So high in heaven no human eye can mark
The thin, swift pinion cleaving through the gray.
Till we awake ill fate can do no ill ;
The resting heart shall not take up again
The heavy load that yet must make it bleed;
For this brief space the loud world's voice is still,
No faintest echo of it brings us pain.
How will it be when we shall sleep indeed?

THOMAS BAILEY ALDRICH.

MY SHELL.

A SHELL upon the sounding sands
    Flashed in the sunshine, where it lay:
Its green disguise I tore; my hands
    Bore the rich treasure-trove away.

Within, the chamber of the pearl
    Blushed like the rose, like opal glowed;
And o'er its domes a cloudy swirl
    Of mimic waves and rainbows flowed.

"Strangely," I said, "the artist-worm
  Has made his palace-lair so bright!
This jeweller, this draughtsman firm,
  Was born and died in eyeless night.

"Deep down in many-monstered caves
  His miracle of beauty throve;
Far from all light, against strong waves,
  A Castle Beautiful he wove.

"Take courage, Soul! Thy labor blind
  The lifting tides may onward bear
To some glad shore, where thou shalt find
  Light, and a Friend to say, 'How fair!'"

THEODORE C. WILLIAMS.

A MYSTERY.

MY eyes are dim with childish tears,
  My heart is idly stirred;
For the same sound is in my ears
  Which in those days I heard.

Thus fares it still in our decay;
  And yet the wiser mind
Mourns less for what age takes away
  Than what it leaves behind.

The blackbird amid leafy trees,
    The lark above the hill,
Let loose their carols when they please,
    Are quiet when they will.

With Nature never do they wage
    A foolish strife ; they see
A happy youth, and their old age
    Is beautiful and free.

But we are pressed by heavy laws ;
    And often, glad no more,
We wear a face of joy because
    We have been glad of yore.

                        WILLIAM WORDSWORTH.

IDEALS.

ANGELS of Growth, of old in that surprise
    Of your first vision, wild and sweet,
        I poured in passionate sighs
        My wish unwise
That ye descend my heart to meet, —
        My heart so slow to rise !

Now thus I pray : Angelic be to hold
In heaven your shining poise afar,
        And to my wishes bold,
        Reply with cold,
Sweet invitation, like a star
        Fixed in the heavens old.

Did ye descend, what were ye more than I
Is 't not by this ye are divine,
    That, native to the sky,
    Ye cannot hie
Downward, and give low hearts the wine
    That should reward the high?

Weak, yet in weakness I no more complain
Of your abiding in your places;
    Oh, still, howe'er my pain
    Wild prayers may rain,
Keep pure on high the perfect graces,
    That stooping could but stain.

Not to content our lowness, but to lure
And lift us to your angelhood,
    Do your surprises pure
    Dawn far and sure
Above the tumult of young blood,
    And starlike there endure.

Wait there, wait and invite me while I climb.
For see, I come! — but slow, but slow!
    Yet ever as your chime,
    Soft and sublime,
Lifts at my feet, they move, they go
    Up the great stair of time.

DAVID A. WASSON.

HEROISM.

RUBY wine is drunk by knaves,
　　Sugar spends to fatten slaves,
Rose and vine-leaf deck buffoons ;
Thunder-clouds are Jove's festoons,
Drooping oft in wreaths of dread
Lightning-knotted round his head.
The hero is not fed on sweets :
Daily his own heart he eats ;
Chambers of the great are jails,
And head-winds right for royal sails.

　　　　　　　RALPH WALDO EMERSON.

ON THE DEATH OF A GREAT MAN.

WHEN from this mortal scene
　　A great soul passes to the vast unknown,
Let not in hopeless grief the spirit groan.
Death comes to all, the mighty and the mean.
If by that death the whole world suffer loss,
This be the proof (and lighter thus our cross),
That he for whom the world doth sorely grieve
Greatly hath blessed mankind in that he once did live.
Then, at the bating breath,
Let men praise Life, nor idly blame dark Death.

　　　　　　　RICHARD WATSON GILDER.

AN INVOCATION.

HIM neither eye has seen, nor ear hath heard;
　　Nor reason, seated in the souls of men,
Though pondering oft on the mysterious word,
Hath e'er revealed his Being to mortal ken.

Only we feel Him: and in aching dreams,
Swift intuitions, pangs of keen delight,
The sudden vision of His glory seems
To sear our souls, dividing the dull night;

And we yearn toward Him.　Beauty, Goodness, Truth;
These three are one, — one life, one thought, one being,
One source of still rejuvenescent youth,
One light for endless and unclouded seeing.

O God, unknown, invisible, secure,
Whose being by dim resemblances we guess,
Who in man's fear and love abidest sure,
Whose power we feel in darkness and confess!

Lead Thou me, God, Law, Reason, Duty, Life!
All names for Thee alike are vain and hollow —
Lead me, for I will follow without strife;
Or, if I strive, still must I blindly follow.

JOHN ADDINGTON SYMONDS.

THE LIFE OF LOVE.

MOST men know love but as a part of life;
    They hide it in some corner of the breast
    Even from themselves; and only when they rest
In the brief pauses of that daily strife
Wherewith the world might else be not so rife,
    They draw it forth (as one draws forth a toy
    To soothe some ardent, kiss-exacting boy)
And hold it up to sister, child, or wife.
    Ah, me! why may not life and love be one?
Why walk we thus alone, when by our side
Love, like a visible god, might be our guide?
How would the marts grow noble, and the street,
Worn like a dungeon floor by weary feet,
    Seem then a golden courtway of the sun!

HENRY TIMROD

THE GOOD SOLDIER.

AND when the wind in the tree-tops roared,
    The soldier asked from the deep, dark grave:
    " Did the banner flutter then?"
" Not so, my hero," the wind replied;
" The fight is done, but, the banner won,
Thy comrades of old have borne it hence,
    Have borne it in triumph hence."
Then the soldier spake from the deep, dark grave:
    " I am content."

Then he heareth the lovers laughing pass,
    And the soldier asks once more:
" Are these not the voices of them that love,
    That love — and remember me? "
" Not so, my hero," the lovers say,
" We are those that remember not;
For the spring has come, and the earth has smiled,
    And the dead must be forgot."
Then the soldier spake from the deep, dark grave:
      " I am content."

SERVIAN FOLK SONG.

WHEN HALF-GODS GO.

GODS fade; but God abides, and in man's heart
    Speaks with the unconquerable cry
  Of energies and hopes that cannot die.
  We feel this sentient self the counterpart
Of some self vaster than the star-girt sky.
    Yea, though our utterance falter; though no art
    By more than sign or signal may impart
    This faith of faiths that lifts our courage high;
Yet there are human duties, human needs,
    Love, charity, self-sacrifice, war
Waged against tyranny, fraud, suffering, crime, —
    These, ever strengthening with the strength of time,
    Exalt man higher than fabled angels are.

JOHN ADDINGTON SYMONDS.

THE UNIVERSAL GOD.

FORASMUCH as all men worship, bow the head
    or bend the knee
Toward a Fate, a Power, a Maker, whom they feel
    yet cannot see,
Source of life and life's Destroyer, Mystery in Mys-
    tery;

Forasmuch as all the winds and all the seas in wild
    acclaim,
All the worlds from outer darkness eddying into light
    and flame,
Roar with rumor of his glory, clang the syllables of
    his name;

Forasmuch as heart and fancy throb with love or
    cower in fear,
Stirred with tremor of his motions, by his shadowing
    shield or spear,
And rebelling or denying every leaf of life is sear;

Forasmuch as they who love, and lean in love upon
    his breast,
Reap the richer bliss of being, drink the dews of a
    deeper rest,
Rise renewed in soul and sinew, greeting life with a
    keener zest, —

I will seek him 'mid the darkness, search his prints
 in the shifting sands,
Kneel beside his feet invisible, crave the touch of his
 viewless hands,
Trust his love, proclaim his splendor trumpet-tongued
 in the listless lands.

GEORGE F. S. ARMSTRONG.

THE MAKING OF MAN.

WHERE is one that, born of woman, altogether
 can escape
From the lower world within him, moods of tiger, or
 of ape?
Man as yet is being made, and ere the crowning Age
 of ages,
Shall not æon after æon pass and touch him into
 shape?

All about him shadow still, but, while the races flower
 and fade,
Prophet-eyes may catch a glory slowly gaining on the
 shade,
Till the peoples all are one, and all their voices blend
 in choric
Hallelujah to the Maker, "It is finished. Man is
 made."

ALFRED TENNYSON.

PRO MORTUIS.

WHAT should a man desire to leave?
　　A flawless work; a noble life;
　Some music harmonized from strife,
Some finished thing, ere the slack hands at eve
　　Drop, should be his to leave.

　One gem of song, defying age;
　　A hard-won fight; a well-worked farm;
　　A law, no guile can twist to harm;
Some tale as our lost Thackeray's, bright, or sage
　　As the just Hallam's page.

　Or, in life's homeliest, meanest spot,
　　With temperate step from year to year
　　To move within his little sphere,
Leaving a pure name to be known, or not, —
　　This is a true man's lot.

　But the imperfect thing, or thought, —
　　The crudities and yeast of youth,
　　The dubious doubt, the twilight truth,
The work that for the passing day was wrought,
　　The schemes that came to naught,

　The sketch half-way 'twixt verse and prose
　　That mocks the finished picture true,
　　The quarry whence the statue grew,
The scaffolding 'neath which the palace rose,
　　The vague abortive throes

And fever-fits of joy or gloom, —
  In kind oblivion let them be !
  Nor has the dead worse foe than he
Who rakes these sweepings of the artist's room,
  And piles them on his tomb.

Ah, 't is but little that the best,
  Frail children of a fleeting hour,
  Can leave of perfect fruit or flower!
Ah, let all else be graciously supprest
  When man lies down to rest !

FRANCIS TURNER PALGRAVE.

BEREAVED.

LET me come in where you sit weeping, — aye,
  Let me, who have not any child to die,
Weep with you for the little one whose love
  I have known nothing of.

The little arms that slowly, slowly loosed
Their pressure round your neck; the hands you used
To kiss, — such arms — such hands I never knew.
  May I not weep with you?

Fain would I be of service, — say something,
Between the tears, that would be comforting, —
But, ah! so sadder than yourselves am I,
  Who have no child to die !

JAMES WHITCOMB RILEY.

THE UNWELCOME GUEST.

WHEN Grief shall come to thee,
  Think not to flee,
For Grief, with steady pace,
Will win the race;
Nor crowd her forth with Mirth,
For at thy hearth,
When Mirth is tired and gone,
Will Grief sit on;
But make of her thy friend,
And in the end
Her counsels will grow sweet,
And, with swift feet,
Three lovelier than she
Will come to thee —
Calm Patience, Courage strong,
And Hope — ere long.

HENRIETTA R. ELIOT.

ANTIPHONOUS.

STROPHE.

AYE, but to die and go we know not where;
  To lie in cold obstruction and to rot;
This sensible warm motion to become
A kneaded clod; and the delighted spirit
To bathe in fiery floods, or to reside
In thrilling regions of rock-ribbed ice;

To be imprisoned in the viewless winds,
And blown with restless violence round about
The pendent world; or to be worse than worst
Of those that lawless and uncertain thoughts
Imagine howling! 'T is too horrible!

WILLIAM SHAKSPERE.

ANTISTROPHE.

Could we be conscious but as dreamers be,
'T were sweet to leave this shifting life of tents
Sunk in the changeless calm of Deity;
Nay, to be mingled with the elements,
The fellow-servant of creative powers,
Partaker in the solemn year's events,
To share the work of busy-fingered hours,
To be night's silent almoner of dew,
To rise again in plants and breathe and grow,
To stream as tides the ocean caverns through,
Or with the rapture of great winds to blow
About earth's shaken coignes, were not a fate
 To leave us all disconsolate.

JAMES RUSSELL LOWELL.

A SABBATH EVENING.

I THANK thee, Lord, that just to-day
 I have not seemed to go astray,
And that to-night the setting sun
Smiles only on my duty done.

Father, not thus thy name I bless
From proud or blind self-righteousness,
Nor that I thus would hope to win
Remission of some wilful sin.

But if to-night I lift my eyes
Unto the all-beholding skies,
And seem to feel within me shine
Some kinship with their calm divine, —

The silent blessing bids me pray,
By this one glad and blameless day
To learn what all my days might be,
If each were holy unto thee.

THEODORE C. WILLIAMS.

THE RISING TIDE.

A N idle man I stroll at eve
        Where move the waters to and fro;
Full soon their added gains will leave
    Small space for me to come and go.

Already in the clogging sand
    I walk with dull, retarded feet;
Yet still is sweet the lessening strand,
    And still the dying light is sweet.

ANONYMOUS.

ENAMOURED ARCHITECT OF AIRY RHYME.

ENAMOURED architect of airy rhyme,
    Build as thou wilt; heed not what each man
        says.
Good souls, but innocent of dreamer's ways,
Will come, and marvel why thou wastest time;
Others, beholding how thy turrets climb
'Twixt theirs and heaven, will hate thee all their days;
But most beware of those who come to praise.
O wondersmith, O worker in sublime
And heaven-sent dreams, let art be all in all;
Build as thou wilt, unspoiled by praise or blame,
Build as thou wilt, and as thy light is given:
Then, if at last the airy structure fall, —
Dissolve, and vanish, — take thyself no shame.
They fail, and they alone, who have not striven.

THOMAS BAILEY ALDRICH.

SPE TREPIDO.

I TREMBLE, not with terror, but with hope,
    As the great day reveals its coming scope:
Never in earlier days, our hearts to cheer,
Have such bright gifts of heaven been brought so near;
Nor ever has been kept the aspiring soul
By space so narrow from so grand a goal.

ARTHUR PENRHYN STANLEY.

A WISH.

WHEN thou, O Death! shalt wait
  Without my gate,
Call not the porter out
With knock and shout;
But still unnoticed bide
The gate beside,
Till Sleep, my oft-time guest,
Doth come in quest
Of me. Quick after her,
Past bolt and bar,
Enter all silently.
Thenceforth for me
The gate thou mayest keep,
That calm-browed Sleep,
So often missed before,
Pass forth no more.

HENRIETTA R. ELIOT.

UNDER GRAY CLOUDS.

UNDER gray clouds some bird will dare to sing,
  No wild, exulting chant, but soft and low;
Under gray clouds the young leaves seek the spring,
  And lurking violets blow;
And waves make idle music on the strand,
  And inland streams have happy words to say,
And children's voices sound across the land,
  Although the clouds are gray.

ANONYMOUS.

THAT BLESSED MOOD.

THAT blessed mood
   In which the burden of the mystery,
In which the heavy and the weary weight
Of all this unintelligible world
Is lightened, — that serene and blessed mood,
In which the affections gently lead us on,
Until, the breath of this corporeal frame,
And even the motion of our human blood,
Almost suspended, we are laid asleep
In body, and become a living soul,
While with an eye made quiet by the power
Of harmony, and the deep power of joy,
We see into the life of things.

WILLIAM WORDSWORTH.

VICTOR.

HE was a hero, fighting all alone,
   A lonesome warrior, — never one more brave, —
   Discreet, considerate, and grave.
   He fought some noble battles; but he gave
No voice to fame, and passed away unknown.

So grandly to occasions did he rise,
   So splendid were the victories he planned,
   That all the world had asked him to command
   Could it his native valor understand: —
He fought himself, and, winning, gained the prize.

IRONQUILL.

ANOTHER YEAR.

THAT this shall be a better year
    Than any passed away,
I dare not at its open door
    To wish or hope or pray.

Not that the years already gone
    Were wearisome and lone;
That so with hope too long deferred
    My heart has timid grown.

Nay, rather that they all have been
    So sweet to me and good,
That if for better I should ask
    'T would seem ingratitude.

And so with things far off and strange
    I do not care to cope,
But look in Memory's face and learn
    What largess I may hope:

Another year of setting suns,
    Of stars by night revealed,
Of springing grass, of tender buds
    By winter's snow concealed.

Another year of summer's glow,
    Of autumn's gold and brown,
Of waving fields, and ruddy fruit
    The branches weighing down.

Another year of happy work,
　Which better is than play;
Of simple cares, and love that grows
　More sweet from day to day.

Another year of baby mirth,
　And childhood's blessed ways,
Of thinker's thought, and prophet's dream,
　And poet's tender lays.

Another year at Beauty's feast,
　At every moment spread,
Of silent hours when grow distinct
　The voices of the dead.

Another year to follow hard
　Where better souls have trod;
Another year of life's delight,
　Another year of God.

　　　　　　　JOHN WHITE CHADWICK.

SOMEDAY.

SOMEDAY:— So many tearful eyes
　　Are watching for thy dawning light;
So many faces toward the skies
　Are weary of the night!

So many failing prayers that reel
　And stagger upward through the storm,
And yearning hands that reach and feel
　No pressure true and warm.

So many hearts whose crimson wine
  Is wasted to a purple stain,
And blurred and streaked with drops of brine
  Upon the lips of Pain.

Oh, come to them, — these weary ones!
  Or, if thou still must bide a while,
Make stronger yet the hope that runs
  Before thy coming smile;

And haste and find them where they wait,
  Let summer winds blow down that way,
And all they long for, soon or late,
  Bring round to them, Someday.

JAMES WHITCOMB RILEY.

THE MORNING STAR.

A SINGLE star, how bright,
    From earth-mists free.
In heaven's deep shrine its image burns!
Star of the morn, my spirit yearns
    To be with thee.

Lord of the desert sky!
    Night's last, lone heir,
Benign thou smilest from on high,
Pure, calm, as if an angel's eye
    Were watching there.

Not wholly vain I deem
    The Magian plan,
That, sphered in thee, a spirit reigns
Who knows this earth, and kindly deigns
    To succor man.

Gone are thy glittering peers,
    Quenched each bright spark,
Save where some pale sun's lingering ghost,
Dull remnant of a scattered host,
    Still spots the dark.

But thou, propitious star,
    Night's youngest born,
Wilt not withdraw thy steady light
Till bursts on yonder snow-clad height
    The rosy morn.

Fair orb! I love to watch
    Thy tranquil ray;
Emblem art thou of Hope that springs
When joys are fled, and dreaming brings
    The better day.

So, when from my life's course
    Its joys are riven,
Rise o'er the death-mists gathering dun,
Herald of an eternal sun,
    Rise, hope of Heaven.

                FREDERIC HENRY HEDGE.

DOUBT AND PRAYER.

THOUGH Sin too oft, when smitten by Thy rod,
    Rail at " Blind Fate " with many a vain " Alas ! "
From sin through sorrow into thee we pass
By that same path our true forefathers trod ;
And let not reason fail me, nor the sod
Draw from my death thy living flower and grass,
Before I learn that Love, which is, and was
My Father, and my Brother, and my God !
Still me with patience ! soften me with grief !
Let blow the trumpet strongly while I pray,
Till this embattled wall of unbelief,
My prison, not my fortress, fall away !
Then, if thou willest, let my day be brief,
So thou wilt strike thy glory through the day.

ALFRED TENNYSON

OLD AND YOUNG.

I.

THEY soon grow old who grope for gold
    In marts where all is bought and sold ;
Who live for self, and on some shelf
In darkened vaults hoard up their pelf,
Cankered and crusted o'er with mould.
For them their youth itself is old.

II.

They ne'er grow old who gather gold
Where spring awakes and flowers unfold;
Where suns arise in joyous skies,
And fill the soul within their eyes.
For them the immortal bards have sung,
For them old age itself is young.

CHRISTOPHER P. CRANCH.

LIGHT OF STARS.

PLAINNESS and clearness without shadow of
stain!
Clearness divine!
Ye Heavens, whose pure dark regions have no sign
Of languor, though so calm; and, though so great,
Are yet untroubled and unpassionate;
Who though so noble share in the world's toil,
And though so tasked keep free from dust and soil, —
I will not say that your mild deeps retain
A tinge, it may be, of their silent pain
Who have longed deeply once, and longed in vain;
But I will rather say that you remain
A world above man's head, to let him see
How boundless might his soul's horizons be,
How vast, yet of what clear transparency;
How it were good to sink there, and breathe free;
How fair a lot to fill
Is left to each man still.

MATTHEW ARNOLD.

THE BETTER WAY.

WHO drives the horses of the sun
 Shall lord it but a day;
Better the lowly deed were done,
 And kept the humble way.

The rust will find the sword of fame;
 The dust will hide the crown;
Ay, none shall nail so high his name
 Time will not tear it down.

The happiest heart that ever beat
 Was in some quiet breast,
That found the common daylight sweet,
 And left to Heaven the rest.
ANONYMOUS.

NO NEED TO WATCH.

LONG looked for was the summer; anxious eyes
 Noted the budding bough, the crocus flame
That told its coming.   Now 'neath autumn skies
The leaves fall slowly, slowly as they came.

There is no need to watch while winter weaves
Fair buds to crown another golden prime,
For something heavier than the autumn leaves
Has hidden eyes that looked for summer time.

The trees shall wake from their forgetful sleep
Unto new blossom and a tender green, —
The countless trees ! — but never one will keep
A little leaf or flower that she has seen.

MARGARET VELEY.

ARRAIGNMENT.

" NOT ye who have stoned, not ye who have smitten
    us," cry
The sad, great souls, as they go out hence into dark,
" Not ye we accuse, though for you was our passion
    borne;
And ye we reproach not who silently passed us by.
We forgive blind eyes and the ears that would not hark,
The careless and causeless hate and the shallow scorn.

" But ye who have seemed to know us, have seen and
    heard;
Who have set us at feasts and have crowned with the
    costly rose;
Who have spread us the purple of praises beneath our
    feet;
Yet guessed not the word that we spake was a living
    word,
Applauding the sound, — we account you as worse
    than foes !
We sobbed you our message; ye said, ' It is song, and
    sweet !' "

HELEN GRAY CONE.

THE CHAMBERED NAUTILUS.

THIS is the ship of pearl which, poets feign,
   Sails the unshadowed main, —
  The venturous bark that flings
On the sweet summer wind its purpled wings
In gulfs enchanted, where the Siren sings,
   And coral reefs lie bare,
Where the cold sea-maids rise to sun their streaming
       hair.

Year after year beheld the silent toil
   That spread his lustrous coil;
  Still, as the spiral grew,
He left the past year's dwelling for the new,
Stole with soft step its shining archway through,
   Built up its idle door,
Stretched in his last-found home, and knew the old no
       more.

Build thee more stately mansions, O my soul,
   As the swift seasons roll!
  Leave thy low-vaulted past!
Let each new temple, nobler than the last,
Shut thee from heaven with a dome more vast,
   Till thou at length art free,
Leaving thine outgrown shell by life's unresting sea!

           OLIVER WENDELL HOLMES.

CHANGE.

SOMETIMES, when after spirited debate
  Of letters or affairs, in thought I go
    Smiling unto myself, and all aglow
With some immediate purpose, and elate
As if my little, trivial scheme were great,
    And what I would so were already so:
    Suddenly I think of her that died, and know,
Whatever friendly or unfriendly fate
    Befall me in my hope or in my pride,
It is all nothing but a mockery,
And nothing can be what it used to be,
    When I could bid my happy life abide,
And build on earth for perpetuity,
    Then, in the deathless days before she died.

WILLIAM D. HOWELLS.

SUB PONDERE CRESCIT.

CAN this be he, whose morning footstep trod
  O'er the green earth as in a regal home?
    Whose voice rang out beneath the skyey dome
    Like the high utterance of a youthful god?
Now with wan looks and eyes that seek the sod,
    Restless and purposeless as ocean foam,
    Across the twilight fields I see him roam
    With shoulders bowed, as shrinking from the
      rod.

Oh, lift the old-time light within thine eyes!
　　Set free the pristine passion from thy tongue!
　　Strength grows with burdens; make an end of
　　　　sighs.
Let thy thoughts soar again their mates among,
　　And, as yon oriole's eager matins rise,
　　Abroad once more be thy strong anthem flung!

THOMAS WENTWORTH HIGGINSON.

SUNSET.

THE children gather at the fence
　　(The gate swings outward to the west)
And watch the purple hills, from whence
　　The father comes for food and rest.
Their lengthened shadows fall behind;
　　Their faces glow the while they wait
To bid him welcome, when they find
　　Their father coming to the gate.

We turn away when sunset fills
　　Our valleys with a glory sweet,
And on the green immortal hills
　　We catch the sound of coming feet;
Our lengthened shadows fall before;
　　Our faces darken as we wait.
Ah, foolish children, who deplore
　　Their Father coming to the gate!

MARY CHACE PECKHAM.

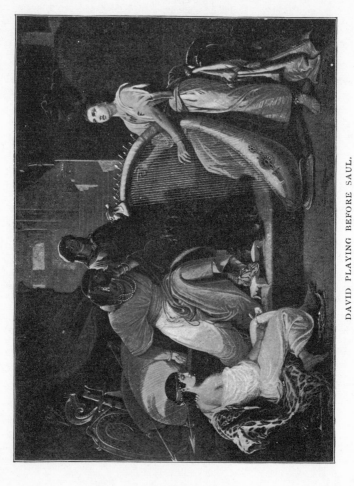

DAVID PLAYING BEFORE SAUL.

From the painting by H. F. Schopin.

THE GREAT ASSURANCE.

A Selection from " Saul."

WHAT, my soul? see thus far and no farther?
    when doors great and small,
Nine-and-ninety, flew ope at our touch, should the
    hundredth appall?
In the least things have faith, yet distrust in the great-
    est of all?
Do I find love so full in my nature, God's ultimate gift,
That I doubt his own love can compete with it? here,
    the parts shift?
Here, the creature surpass the Creator, the end, what
    Began? —
Would I fain in my impotent yearning do all for this
    man,
And dare doubt He alone shall not help him, who yet
    alone can?
Would it ever have entered my mind, the bare will,
    much less power,
To bestow on this Saul what I sang of, the marvellous
    dower
Of the life he was gifted and filled with? to make such
    a soul,
Such a body, and then such an earth for insphering
    the whole?
And doth it not enter my mind (as my warm tears
    attest)
These good things being given, to go on, and give one
    more, the best?

Ay, to save and redeem and restore him, maintain at
    the height
This perfection, — succeed with life's dayspring,
    death's minute of night?

.   .   .   .   .   .

I believe it! 't is thou, God, that givest, 't is I who
    receive:
In the first is the last, in thy will is my power to
    believe.
All's one gift: thou canst grant it, moreover, as
    prompt to my prayer
As I breathe out this breath, as I open these arms to
    the air.
                    ROBERT BROWNING.

"THE THINGS THAT ARE MORE EXCELLENT."

AS we wax older on this earth,
    Till many a toy that charmed us seems
Emptied of beauty, stripped of worth,
    And mean as dust and dead as dreams, —
For gauds that perished, shows that passed,
    Some recompense the Fates have sent:
Thrice lovelier shine the things that last,
    The things that are more excellent.

Naught nobler is than to be free;
    The stars of heaven are free because
In amplitude of liberty
    Their joy is to obey the laws.

From servitude to freedom's *name*
   Free thou thy mind in bondage pent;
Depose the fetich, and proclaim
   The things that are more excellent.

To dress, to call, to dine, to break
   No canon of the social code,
The little laws that lackeys make,
   The futile decalogue of Mode, —
How many a soul for these things lives,
   With pious passion, grave intent!
While Nature, careless handed, gives
   The things that are more excellent.

To hug the wealth ye cannot use,
   And lack the riches all may gain, —
Oh, blind and wanting wit to choose,
   Who house the chaff and burn the grain!
And still doth life with starry towers
   Lure to the bright, divine ascent! —
Be yours the things ye would: be ours
   The things that are more excellent.

The grace of friendship, — mind and heart
   Linked with their fellow heart and mind;
The gains of science, gifts of art;
   The sense of oneness with our kind;
The thirst to know and understand,
   A large and liberal discontent, —
These are the goods in life's rich hand,
   The things that are more excellent.

In faultless rhythm the ocean rolls,
　　A rapturous silence thrills the skies;
And on this earth are lovely souls,
　　That softly look with aidful eyes.
Though dark, O God, thy course and track,
　　I think thou must at least have meant
That naught which lives should wholly lack
　　The things that are more excellent.

WILLIAM WATSON.

THEOLOGY IN EXTREMIS.

OFT in the pleasant summer years,
　　Reading the tales of days bygone,
I have mused on the story of human tears,
　　All that man unto man has done,
Massacre, torture, and black despair;
Reading it all in my easy-chair.

Passionate prayer for a minute's life,
　　Tortured crying for death as rest,
Husband pleading for child or wife,
　　Pitiless stroke upon tender breast,—
Was it all real as that I lay there
Lazily stretched on my easy-chair?

Could I believe in those hard old times,
　　Here in this safe, luxurious age?
Were the horrors invented to season rhymes,

Or truly is man so fierce in his rage?
What could I suffer and what could I dare,
I who was bred to that easy-chair?

They were my fathers, the men of yore,
   Little they recked of a cruel death;
They would dip their hands in a heretic's gore;
   They stood and burnt for a rule of faith.
What would I burn for, and whom not spare,
I who had faith in an easy-chair?

Now do I see old tales are true,
   Here in the clutch of a savage foe;
Now shall I know what my fathers knew,
   Bodily anguish and bitter woe,
Naked and bound in the strong sun's glare,
Far from my civilized easy-chair.

Now have I tasted and understood
   That old-world feeling of mortal hate;
For the eyes all round us are hot with blood:
   They will kill us coolly, — they do but wait;
While I, I would sell ten lives, at least,
For one fair stroke at that devilish priest.

Just in return for the kick he gave,
   Bidding me call on the prophet's name;
Even a dog by this may save
   Skin from the knife and soul from the flame;
My soul! if he can let the prophet burn it, —
But life is sweet if a word may earn it.

A bullock's death, and at thirty years !
   Just one phrase and a man gets off it;
Look at that mongrel clerk in his tears,
   Whining aloud the name of the prophet!
Only a formula easy to patter,
And, God Almighty, what *can* it matter?

" Matter enough," will my comrade say,
   Praying aloud here close at my side,
" Whether you mourn in despair alway,
   Cursed forever by Christ denied ;
Or whether you suffer a minute's pain,
All the reward of heaven to gain."

Not for a moment faltereth he,
   Sure of the promise and pardon of sin ;
Thus did the martyrs die, I see,
   Little to lose and muckle to win ;
Death means heaven, — he longs to receive it.
But what shall I do if I don't believe it?

Life is pleasant, and friends may be nigh,
   Fain would I speak one word and be spared ;
Yet I could be silent and cheerfully die,
   If I were only sure God cared ;
If I had faith, and were only certain
That light is behind that terrible curtain.

But what if he listeth nothing at all
   Of words a poor wretch in his terror may say ?
That mighty God who created all

To labor and live their appointed day, —
Who stoops not either to bless or ban,
Weaving the woof of an endless plan?

He is the Reaper and binds the sheaf;
   Shall not the season its order keep?
Can it be changed by a man's belief?
   Millions of harvests still to reap;
Will God reward, if I die for a creed,
Or will he but pity, and sow more seed?

Surely he pities who made the brain,
   When breaks that mirror of memories sweet,
When the hard blow falleth, and never again
   Nerve shall quiver nor pulse shall beat.
Bitter the vision of vanishing joys;
Surely he pities when man destroys.

Here stand I on the ocean's brink;
   Who hath brought news of the further shore?
How shall I cross it?   Sail or sink,
   One thing is sure, I return no more;
Shall I find haven, or aye shall I be
Tossed in the depths of a shoreless sea?

They tell fair tales of a far-off land,
   Of love rekindled, of forms renewed;
There may I only touch one hand,
   Here life's ruin will little be rued;
But the hand I have pressed and the voice I have
      heard,
   To lose them forever, and all for a word!

Now do I feel that my heart must break
  All for one glimpse of a woman's face;
Swiftly the slumbering memories wake
  Odor and shadow of hour and place;
One bright ray through the darkening past
Leaps from the lamp as it brightens last,

Showing me summer in western land
  Now, as the cool breeze murmureth
In leaf and flower—and here I stand
  In this plain all bare save the shadow of death;
Leaving my life in its full noonday,
And no one to know why I flung it away.

Why?   Am I bidding for glory's roll?
  I shall be murdered and clean forgot;
Is it a bargain to save my soul?
  God, whom I trust in, bargains not;
Yet for the honor of English race,
May I not live or endure disgrace.

Ay, but the word, if I could have said it,
  I by no terrors of hell perplext!
Hard to be silent and have no credit
  From man in this world, or reward in the next;
None to bear witness and reckon the cost
Of the name that is saved by the life that is lost.

I must be gone to the crowd untold
  Of men by the cause which they served unknown,
Who moulder in myriad graves of old;

Never a story and never a stone
Tells of the martyrs who die like me,
Just for the pride of the old countree.

ALFRED LYALL.

THE TWO MYSTERIES.

WE know not what it is, dear, this sleep so deep
and still;
The folded hands, the awful calm, the cheek so pale
and chill;
The lids that will not lift again, though we may call
and call;
The strange, white solitude of peace that settles
over all.

We know not what it means, dear, this desolate heart-
pain;
This dread to take our daily way, and walk in it again;
We know not to what other sphere the loved who
leave us go,
Nor why we're left to wonder still, nor why we do not
know.

But this we know: Our loved and dead, if they should
come this day —
Should come and ask us, "What is life?" not one of
us could say.
Life is a mystery as deep as ever death can be;
Yet oh, how dear it is to us, this life we live and see!

Then might they say, — these vanished ones, — and
    blessèd is the thought :
" So death is sweet to us, beloved ! though we may
    show you naught ;
We may not to the quick reveal the mystery of death, —
Ye cannot tell us, if ye would, the mystery of breath."

The child who enters life comes not with knowledge
    or intent ;
So those who enter death must go as little children
    sent.
Nothing is known.   But I believe that God is over-
    head ;
And as life is to the living, so death is to the dead.

                      MARY MAPES DODGE.

EPITAPH FOR A SAILOR BURIED ASHORE.

HE who but yesterday would roam
    Careless as clouds and currents range,
In homeless wandering most at home,
    Inhabiter of change ;

Who wooed the West to win the East,
    And named the stars from North to South,
And felt the zest of freedom's feast
    Familiar in his mouth ;

Who found a faith in stranger speech
   And fellowship in foreign hands,
And had within his eager reach
   The relish of all lands, —

How circumscribed a plot of earth
   Keeps now his restless footsteps still,
Whose wish was wide as ocean's girth,
   Whose will the water's will!

CHARLES G. D. ROBERTS.

OPPORTUNITY.

THIS I beheld or dreamed it in a dream : —
   There spread a cloud of dust along a plain;
And underneath the cloud, or in it, raged
A furious battle, and men yelled, and swords
Shocked upon swords and shields. A prince's banner
Wavered, then staggered backward hemmed by foes.
A craven hung along the battle's edge,
And thought, " Had I a sword of keener steel —
That blue blade that the king's son bears — but this
Blunt thing — " He snapt and flung it from his hand,
And lowering crept away and left the field.
Then came the king's son, wounded, sore bestead,
And weaponless, and saw the broken sword,
Hilt buried in the dry and trodden sand,
And ran, and snatched it, and with battle-shout
Lifted afresh he hewed his enemy down,
And saved a great cause that heroic day.

EDWARD ROWLAND SILL.

EVER WOMANLY.

SET her among the angels! let her shine a star!
   Nay, call her woman, never more divine
Than when she walks the levels where our human
            longings are,
   And lightens up the prison where we pine.

Be angel to my worship! be star my steps to lead
   From earth's deep gloom to thy radiance above!
The daily inspiration of thine influence I need;
   But, oh, be simply woman to my love!

WILLIAM ROSCOE THAYER.

RENASCENCE.

I MUSE in shadow, knowing naught
   How deep this twilight sad and dark
May gloom before the dawn is fraught
   With light for some full-throated lark.

I am content: the night may fall
   And brood with more than ebon wing,
But at the appointed time and call
   The sun shall rise, the lark shall sing.

JOHN H. BONER.

BUILDING THE FUTURE.

O TRUTH! O Freedom! how are ye still born
    In the rude stable, in the manger nursed!
What humble hands unbar those gates of morn,
    Through which the splendors of the New Day
        burst!

Who is it will not dare himself to trust?
    Who is it hath not strength to stand alone?
Who is it thwarts and bilks the inward *Must?*
    He and his works like sand from earth are blown.

Shall we not heed the lesson taught of old,
    And by the Present's lips repeated still,
In our own simple manhood to be bold,
    Fortressed in conscience and impregnable will?

We stride the river daily at its spring,
    Nor, in our childish thoughtlessness, foresee
What myriad vassal streams shall tribute bring,
    How like an equal it shall greet the sea.

O small beginnings, ye are great and strong,
    Based on a faithful heart and weariless brain!
Ye build the future fair, ye conquer wrong,
    Ye earn the crown and wear it not in vain.

                    JAMES RUSSELL LOWELL.

WHAT IS TO COME.

WHAT is to come we know not; but we know
    That what has been was good, — was good to
        show,
Better to hide, and best of all to bear.
We are the masters of the days that were.
We have lived, we have loved, we have suffered —
        even so.

Shall we not take the ebb who had the flow?
Life was our friend.   Now, if it be our foe,
Dear, — though it spoil and break us, — need we care
    What is to come?

Let the great winds their worst and wildest blow,
Or the gold weather round us mellow slow;
We have fulfilled ourselves, and we can dare,
And we can conquer, though we may not share
In the rich quiet of the afterglow,
    What is to come.
                WILLIAM E. HENLEY.

BEYOND THE CLOUDS.

WILD, wandering clouds, that none can tame,
    Shake the sweet rain out to the ground!
The sky beyond is still the same,
    Beyond you hangs the clear blue round.

Come, Night, and bind the world again
　With sevenfold darkness as with bars!
Upward, the path will still be plain, —
　The pathway lighted by the stars.

WILLIAM BRIGHTY RANDS.

SUNRISE NEVER FAILS.

UPON the sadness of the sea
　　The sunset broods regretfully;
From the far, lonely spaces, slow
Withdraws the wistful afterglow.

So out of life the splendor dies,
So darken all the happy skies,
So gathers twilight cold and stern;
But overhead the planets burn.

And up the east another day
Shall chase the bitter dark away.
What though our eyes with tears be wet?
The sunrise never failed us yet.

The blush of dawn may yet restore
Our light and hope and joys once more.
Sad soul, take comfort, nor forget
That sunrise never failed us yet!

CELIA THAXTER.

TO WALK WITH GOD.

To walk with God! — to feel no more alone
　　Amid the Vast, wherein I breathed in fear;
To cry for help no more, nor utter moan,
　　So sure that he who made and guides is near;
Whether the tempest drive against my face,
　　Or Summer's lavish blossom strew my way,
To miss his presence not in any place,
　　　　By night or day, —

How sweet it is! how different from my lot
　　Through those long years of doubt and grief and
　　　　pain,
Of love that looked for love and found it not,
　　Of thought that climbed for light and climbed in
　　　　vain!
How different from the dread perplexity
　　Wherein with trembling feet the waste I trod,
Not knowing when the bolt might fall on me
　　　　Of Fate or God!

How sweet it is — not holding now the creed
　　Which dwarfs the Maker to his creature's height,
Or to his hand imputes a baffled deed,
　　Or doubts the certain victory of his might,
Or falters in allegiance to his love —
　　To cast away all fear of hovering doom,
And onward, trustful of his mercy, move,
　　　　In sun or gloom!

To walk with God!— to drink with fearless heart
    The beauty and the marvel of his earth;
To dote upon the wings that round me dart;
    To revel in the summer's reinless mirth,
Or bear with patient breast the winter's woe,
       And shrink not from misfortune's bitterest breath,
Still trusting Good through every throb and throe
       Of life or death.
          GEORGE F. S. ARMSTRONG.

NEARING THE END.

THE voyage draws near its end; the westering sun
    Shorn of its noonday heat, yet full of light,
Marks the smooth waters with a glory bright,
Richer than pearly gleams from morning won.

The shore, which when our voyage was but begun
    Lay so remote beyond even thought's far flight,
    Now on the horizon lifts itself to sight:
Sees it our failure, or our work well done?

Something perhaps of both the voyage has brought,
    Of our large venture something must avail;
    For dreams of youth we have the faith of age,

By knowledge chastened, by experience taught!
    And now the time has come to shorten sail;
    The tranquil harbor calls to anchorage!
          SAMUEL LONGFELLOW

THE GLORIOUS COMPANY.

" FACES, faces, faces of the streaming, marching
        surge,
Streaming on the weary road, toward the awful steep,
Whence your glow and glory, as ye set to that sharp
        verge,
Faces lit as sunlit stars, shining as ye sweep?

" Whence this wondrous radiance that ye somehow
        catch and cast,
Faces rapt, that one discerns 'mid the dusky press
Herding in dull wonder, gathering fearful to the Vast?
Surely all is dark before, night of nothingness!"

" Lo, the Light!" they answer. "O the pure, the
        pulsing Light,
Beating like a heart of life, like a heart of love;
Soaring, searching, filling all the breadth and depth
        and height,
Welling, whelming with its peace worlds below,
        above!"

"O my soul, how art thou to that living Splendor
        blind,
Sick with thy desire to see even as these men see!
Yet to look upon them is to know that God hath
        shined:
Faces lit as sunlit stars, be all my light to me!"

                                HELEN GRAY CONE.

THE TWO ARMIES.

A S Life's unending column pours,
　　Two marshalled hosts are seen,—
Two armies on the trampled shores
　　That Death flows black between.

One marches to the drumbeat's roll,
　　The wide-mouthed clarion's bray,
And bears, upon a crimson scroll,
　　"Our glory is to slay."

One moves in silence by the stream,
　　With sad, yet watchful eyes,
Calm as the patient planet's gleam
　　That walks the clouded skies.

Along its front no sabres shine,
　　No blood-red pennons wave;
Its banner bears the single line,
　　"Our duty is to save."

OLIVER WENDELL HOLMES.

SUPERSTITION.

A MID the verdure on the prairies wide,
　　There stretches o'er the undulating floor,
As on the edges of an ocean-shore,
From east to west, half buried, side by side,

A chain of bowlders that the icy tide
  Of glacial epoch, centuries before,
  From arctic hills superfluously bore,
And left in southern summers to abide.

So on the landscape of our times is seen
    The rough *débris* of error's old moraines.
    The superstitions of a thousand creeds,
Half-buried, peer above the waving green;
    But kindly time will cover their remains
    Beneath a sod of noble thoughts and deeds.

                                        IRONQUILL.

INTIMATION.

ONLY — but this is rare —
    When a beloved hand is laid in ours,
When, jaded with the rush and glare
Of the interminable hours,
Our eyes can in another's eyes read clear,
When our world-deafened ear
Is by the tones of a loved voice caress'd, —
  A bolt is shot back somewhere in our breast,
And a lost pulse of feeling stirs again;
The eye sinks inward, and the heart lies plain,
And what we mean we say, and what we would we
            know.
A man becomes aware of his life's flow,
And hears its winding murmur, and he sees
The meadow where it glides, the sun, the breeze.

And there arrives a lull in the hot race
Wherein he doth forever chase
That flying and elusive shadow, Rest.
An air of coolness plays upon his face,
And an unwonted calm pervades his breast.
    And then he thinks he knows
The Hills where his life rose,
And the Sea where it goes.
                            MATTHEW ARNOLD

ANGEL OF PAIN.

ANGEL of Pain, I think thy face
    Will be, in all the heavenly place,
The sweetest face that I shall see,
The swiftest face to smile on me.
All other angels faint and tire;
Joy wearies, and forsakes Desire;
Hope falters, face to face with Fate,
And dies because it cannot wait;
And Love cuts short each loving day,
Because fond hearts cannot obey
That subtlest law which measures bliss
By what it is content to miss.
But thou, O loving, faithful Pain, —
Hated, reproached, rejected, slain, —
Dost only closer cling and bless
In sweeter, stronger steadfastness.
Dear, patient angel, to thine own
Thou comest, and art never known

Till, late, in some lone twilight place,
The light of thy transfigured face
Shines sudden out, and, speechless, they
Know they have walked with God all day.

ANONYMOUS.

TOGETHER.

SWEET hand that, held in mine,
  Seems the one thing I cannot live without,
The soul's one anchorage in this storm and doubt,
    I take thee as the sign

    Of sweeter days in store
For life, and more than life, when life is done,
And thy soft pressure leads me gently on
    To heaven's own Evermore.

    I have not much to say,
Nor any words that fit such fond request:
Let my blood speak to thine, and bear the rest
    Some silent, heartward way.

    Thrice blest the faithful hand
Which saves e'en while it blesses: hold me fast;
Let me not go beneath the floods at last,
    So near the better land.

    Sweet hand that, thus in mine,
Seems the one thing I cannot live without,
My heart's one anchor in life's storm and doubt,
    Take this and make me thine.

JAMES ANTHONY FROUDE (?)

LOSSES.

UPON the white sea sand
　　There sat a pilgrim band,
Telling the losses that their lives had known,
　　While evening waned away
　　From breezy cliff and bay,
And the strong tides went out with weary moan.

　　Some talked of vanished gold;
　　Some, of proud honors told;
Some spoke of friends that were their trust no more;
　　And one, of a green grave
　　Beside a foreign wave,
That made him sit so lonely on the shore.

　　But when their tales were done,
　　There spake among them one,
A stranger, seeming from all sorrow free:
　　" Sad losses have ye met,
　　But mine is heavier yet,
For a believing heart hath gone from me."

　　" Alas," those pilgrims said,
　　" For the living and the dead;
For fortune's cruelty and love's sure cross;
　　For the wrecks of land and sea!
　　But, however it came to thee,
Thine, stranger, is life's last and heaviest loss."

FRANCES BROWN.

CALVARY.

IF he could doubt on his triumphant cross,
　How much more I, in the defeat and loss
Of seeing all my selfish dreams fulfilled,
Of having lived the very life I willed,
Of being all that I desired to be?
My God, my God! why hast thou forsaken me?

WILLIAM D. HOWELLS.

IF ENDLESS SLEEP.

AND if there be no meeting past the grave,
　If all is darkness, silence, yet 't is rest.
Be not afraid, ye waiting hearts that weep,
For God still giveth his beloved sleep.
And if an endless sleep he wills, — so best.

MRS. THOMAS H. HUXLEY.

THE CHILD IN THE MIDST.

GREAT, wide, beautiful, wonderful World,
　With the wonderful water round you curled,
And the wonderful grass upon your breast, —
World, you are beautifully drest.

The wonderful air is over me,
And the wonderful wind is shaking the tree;
It walks on the water, and whirls the mills,
And talks to itself on the tops of the hills.

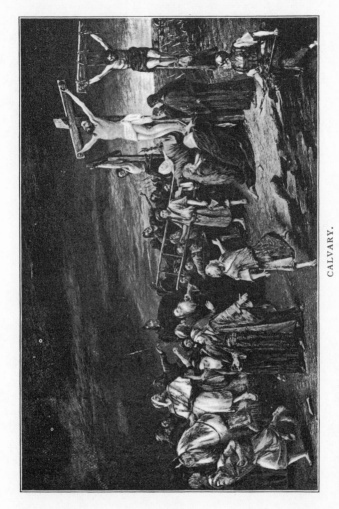

CALVARY.

From the painting by Gerome.

You friendly Earth! how far do you go,
With the wheatfields that nod, and the rivers that
      flow;
With cities, and gardens, and cliffs, and isles,
And people upon you for thousands of miles?

Ah, you are so great and I am so small,
I tremble to think of you, World, at all;
And yet, when I said my prayers to-day,
A whisper inside me seemed to say,
"You are more than the Earth, though you are such
      a dot:
You can love and think, and the Earth cannot!"

                WILLIAM BRIGHTY RANDS.

EPILOGUE.

AT the midnight, in the silence of the sleep-time,
    When you set your fancies free,
Will they pass to where — by death, fools think, im-
      prisoned —
Low he lies who once so loved you, whom you love so,
    — Pity me?

Oh to love so, be so loved, yet so mistaken!
    What had I on earth to do
With the slothful, with the mawkish, the unmanly?
Like the aimless, helpless, hopeless, did I drivel
    — Being — who?

One who never turned his back, but marched breast
        forward,
    Never doubted clouds would break,
Never dreamed, though right were worsted, wrong
        would triumph,
Held we fall to rise, are baffled to fight better,
    Sleep to wake.

No, at noontide, in the bustle of man's work-time,
    Greet the unseen with a cheer!
Bid him forward, breast and back as either should be,
"Strive and thrive!" cry, "Speed, fight on, fare ever
    There as here!"

                    Robert Browning.

A SONG OF THE CRUISE.

OH, the sun and the rain, and the rain and the sun!
    There 'll be sunshine again when the tempest is
    done;
And the storm will beat back when the shining is
    past,
But in some happy haven we'll anchor at last.
      Then murmur no more,
      In lull or in roar,
But smile and be brave till the voyage is o'er.

Oh, the rain and the sun, and the sun and the rain!
When the tempest is done, then the sunshine again;

And in rapture we 'll ride through the stormiest gales,
For God's hand 's on the helm, and his breath in the
      sails.
    Then murmur no more,
     In lull or in roar,
But smile and be brave till the voyage is o'er.

JAMES WHITCOMB RILEY

ODE TO DUTY.

STERN daughter of the voice of God!
   O duty! if that name thou love
Who art a light to guide, a rod
To check the erring and reprove;
Thou who art victory and law
When empty terrors overawe;
From vain temptations dost set free;
And calm'st the weary strife of frail humanity!

There are who ask not if thine eye
Be on them; who, in love and truth,
Where no misgiving is, rely
Upon the genial sense of youth:
Glad hearts! without reproach or blot,
Who do thy work and know it not;
May joy be theirs while life shall last!
And thou, if they should totter, teach them to stand
    fast!

Serene will be our days, and bright
And happy will our nature be,
When love is an unerring light,
And joy its own security.
And blest are they who in the main
This faith, even now, do entertain;
Live in the spirit of this creed,
Yet find that other strength, according to their need.

I, loving freedom, and untried,
No sport of every random gust,
Yet being to myself a guide,
Too blindly have reposed my trust;
Full oft, when in my heart was heard
Thy timely mandate, I deferred
The task imposed, from day to day;
But thee I now would serve more strictly, if I may.

Through no disturbance of my soul,
Or strong compunction in me wrought,
I supplicate for thy control,
But in the quietness of thought.
Me this unchartered freedom tires;
I feel the weight of chance desires;
My hopes no more must change their name;
I long for a repose which ever is the same.

Yet not the less would I throughout
Still act according to the voice
Of my own wish, and feel past doubt
That my submissiveness was choice,

Not seeking in the school of pride
For precepts over-dignified,
Denial and restraint I prize
No farther than they breed a second Will more wise.

Stern lawgiver! yet thou dost wear
The Godhead's most benignant grace;
Nor know we any thing so fair
As is the smile upon thy face;
Flowers laugh before thee on their beds,
And fragrance in thy footing treads;
Thou dost preserve the stars from wrong,
And the most ancient heavens, through thee, are fresh
    and strong.

To humbler functions, awful power!
I call thee: I myself commend
Unto thy guidance from this hour.
Oh, let my weakness have an end!
Give unto me, made lowly wise,
The spirit of self-sacrifice;
The confidence of reason give;
And in the light of truth, thy bondman let me live!

WILLIAM WORDSWORTH.

CONSCIENCE.

JUDGE me not as I judge myself, O Lord!
    Show me some mercy, or I may not live;
Let the good in me go without reward;
    Forgive the evil I cannot forgive!

WILLIAM D. HOWELLS.

A LOW ESTATE.

THIS is the night when I must die,
　　And great Orion walketh high
In silent glory overhead:
He 'll set just after I am dead.

A week this night, I 'm in my grave;
Orion walketh o'er the wave:
Down in the dark, damp earth I lie,
While he doth march in majesty.

A few weeks hence and spring will come;
The earth will bright array put on
Of daisy and of primrose bright,
And everything which loves the light.

And some one to my child will say,
"You 'll soon forget that you could play
Beethoven; let us hear a strain
From that slow movement once again."

And so she 'll play that melody,
While I, unconscious, here do lie,
Dead to them all, forever dead,
The churchyard clay dense overhead.

I once did think there might be mine
One friendship perfect and divine;
Alas! that dream dissolved in tears
Before I 'd counted twenty years.

For I was ever commonplace;
Of genius never had a trace ;
My thoughts the world have never fed,
Mere echoes of the book last read.

Those whom I know I cannot blame ;
If they are cold, I am the same.
How could they ever show to me
More than a common courtesy?

There is no deed which I have done,
There is no love which I have won,
To make them for a moment grieve
That I this night their earth must leave.

Thus moaning at the break of day,
A man upon his deathbed lay ;
A moment more and all was still ;
The Morning Star came o'er the hill.

But when the dawn lay on his face,
It kindled an immortal grace,
As if in death that Life were shown
Which lives not in the great alone.

Orion sank down in the west
Just as he sank into his rest ;
I closed in solitude his eyes,
And watched him till the sun's uprise.

W. HALE WHITE.

ALL 'S WELL.

SWEET-VOICÈD Hope, thy fine discourse
    Foretold not half life's good to me;
Thy painter, Fancy, hath not force
    To show how sweet it is to be!
        Thy witching dream
        And pictured scheme
To match the fact still want the power;
        Thy promise brave
        From birth to grave
Life's boon may beggar in an hour.

Ask and receive, — 't is sweetly said.
    Yet what to plead for know I not;
For Wish is worsted, Hope o'ersped,
    And aye to thanks returns my thought.
        If I would pray,
        I 've naught to say
But this, that God may be God still;
        For him to live
        Is still to give,
And sweeter than my wish his will.

O wealth of life beyond all bound!
    Eternity each moment given!
What plummet may the present sound?
    Who promises a *future* heaven?
        Or glad or grieved,
        Oppressed, relieved,

In blackest night or brightest day,
    Still pours the flood
    Of golden good,
And more than heartfull fills me aye.

My wealth is common; I possess
    No petty province, but the whole;
What's mine alone is mine far less
    Than treasure shared by every soul.
      Talk not of store,
      Millions or more, —
Of values which the purse may hold, —
      But this divine!
      I own the mine
Whose grains outweigh a planet's gold.

I have a stake in every star,
    In every beam that fills the day;
All hearts of men my coffers are,
    My ores arterial tides convey;
      The fields, the skies,
      And sweet replies
Of thought to thought are my gold-dust, —
      The oaks, the brooks,
      And speaking looks
Of lovers' faith and friendship's trust.

Love's youngest tides joy-brimming flow
    For him who lives above all years,
Who all-immortal makes the Now,
    And is not ta'en in Time's arrears;

His life 's a hymn
The seraphim
Might hark to hear or help to sing,
And to his soul
The boundless whole
Its bounty all doth daily bring.

"All mine is thine," the sky-soul saith;
"The wealth I am must thou become:
Richer and richer, breath by breath, —
Immortal gain, immortal room!"
And since all his
Mine also is,
Life's gift outruns my fancies far,
And drowns the dream
In larger stream,
As morning drinks the morning star.

DAVID A. WASSON.

AD MAJOREM DEI GLORIAM.

THY glory alone, O God, be the end of all that I
say;
Let it shine in every deed, let it kindle the prayers that
I pray;
Let it burn in my innermost soul, till the shadow of
self pass away,
And the light of thy glory, O God, be unveiled in the
dawning of day.

FREDERICK GEORGE SCOTT.

GOTT UND WELT.

Translated from Johann Wolfgang Goethe.

TO Him who from eternity, self-stirred,
   Himself hath made by His creative word !
To Him, Supreme, who causeth faith to be,
Trust, love, hope, power, and endless energy !
To Him who, seek to name Him as we will,
Unknown, within Himself, abideth still !

Strain ear and eye, till sight and sense be dim,
Thou 'lt find but faint similitudes of Him.
Yea, and thy spirit, in her flight of flame,
Still strives to gauge the symbol and the name.
Charmed and compelled, thou climb'st from height to
               height,
And round thy path the world shines wondrous bright;
Time, space, and size, and distance cease to be,
And every step is fresh infinity.

What were the God who sat outside to scan
The spheres that 'neath His fingers circling ran?
God dwells within, and moves the world and moulds,
Himself and Nature in one form enfolds;
Thus all that lives in Him, and breathes, and is,
Shall ne'er His puissance, ne'er His spirit miss.

The soul of man, too, is an universe;
Whence follows it that race with race concurs

In naming all it knows of good and true
God, — yea, its own God; and, with homage due,
Surrenders to His sway both earth and heaven;
Hears Him, and loves, where place for love is given.

JOHN ADDINGTON SYMONDS.

HOW BEAUTIFUL TO BE ALIVE!

HOW beautiful it is to be alive!
    To wake each morn as if the Maker's grace
Did us afresh from nothingness derive,
That we might sing, How happy is our case!
How beautiful it is to be alive!

To read in some good book until we feel
Love for the one who wrote it; then to kneel
Close unto Him whose love our souls will shrive,
While every moment's joy doth more reveal
How beautiful it is to be alive.

Rather to go without what might increase
Our worldly standing than our souls deprive
Of frequent speech with God, or than to cease
To feel, through having lost our health and peace,
How beautiful it is to be alive.

Not to forget, when pain and grief draw nigh,
Into the ocean of time past to dive
For memories of God's mercies; or to try
To bear all nobly, hoping still to cry,
How beautiful it is to be alive.

Thus ever, towards man's height of nobleness,
Striving some new progression to contrive;
Till, just as any other friend's, we press
Death's hand, and, having died, feel none the less
How beautiful it is to be alive.

HENRY SEPTIMUS SUTTON.

THE HEAVENS DECLARE THY GLORY.

THIS world I deem
But a beautiful dream
Of shadows that are not what they seem,
Where visions rise,
Giving dim surmise
Of the things that shall meet our waking eyes.

Arm of the Lord!
Creating Word!
Whose glory the silent skies record
Where stands thy name
In scrolls of flame
On the firmament's high-shadowing frame,

I gaze o'erhead,
Where thy hand hath spread
For the waters of heaven that crystal bed,
And stored the dew
In its deeps of blue,
Which the fires of the sun come tempered through.

I gaze aloof
On the tissued roof,
Where time and space are the warp and woof,
Which the King of kings
As a curtain flings
O'er the dreadfulness of eternal things, —

A tapestried tent
To shade us meant
From the bare, everlasting firmament,
Where the blaze of the skies
Comes soft to our eyes
Through a veil of mystical imageries.

But could I see
As in truth they be
The glories of heaven that encompass me,
I should lightly hold
The tissued fold
Of that marvellous curtain of blue and gold.

THOMAS WHYTEHEAD.

SAVED BY HOPE.

WHAT can we do to whom the unbeholden
    Hangs in a night with which we cannot cope?
What but look sunward, and with faces golden
    Speak to each other softly of a hope?

FREDERIC W. H. MYERS.

AULD LANG SYNE.

IT singeth low in every heart,
 We hear it each and all, —
A song of those who answer not,
 However we may call;
They throng the silence of the breast,
 We see them as of yore, —
The kind, the brave, the true, the sweet,
 Who walk with us no more.

'T is hard to take the burden up,
 When these have laid it down;
They brightened all the joy of life,
 They softened every frown;
But, oh, 't is good to think of them
 When we are troubled sore!
Thanks be to God that such have been,
 Although they are no more!

More homelike seems the vast unknown,
 Since they have entered there;
To follow them were not so hard,
 Wherever they may fare;
They cannot be where God is not,
 On any sea or shore;
Whate'er betides, Thy love abides,
 Our God, for evermore.

JOHN WHITE CHADWICK.

MY STAR.

Written when an open window at night furnished the writer
habitually her only glimpse of the outer world.

A SCRAP of sky
    Have I;
Great wealth it is to me,
    Such glorious things
Therein I see.

The morning star
Comes from afar;
For me it shines so bright,
Brings me a heavenly light,
Sent from my Lord above,
That I may trust his love.

                MARY OSGOOD.

THE ANSWER.

"ALLAH, Allah!" cried the sick man, racked with
        pain the long night through;
Till with prayer his heart grew tender, till his lips like
    honey grew.

But at morning came the Tempter; said, "Call louder,
    child of pain!
See if Allah ever hears, or answers, 'Here am I,'
    again!"

Like a stab the cruel cavil through his brain and
    pulses went;
To his heart an icy coldness, to his brain a darkness
    sent.

Then before him stands Elias; says, "My child, why
    thus dismayed?
Dost repent thy former fervor?   Is thy soul of prayer
    afraid?"

"Ah!" he cried, "I 've called so often; never heard
    the 'Here am I!'
And I thought, God will not pity, will not turn on me
    his eye."

Then the grave Elias answered: "God said, 'Rise,
    Elias; go,
Speak to him, the sorely tempted; lift him from his
    gulf of woe.

"'Tell him that his very longing is itself an answer-
    ing cry;
That his prayer, "Come, gracious Allah," is my
    answer, "Here am I."'"

Every inmost aspiration is God's angel undefiled;
And in every "O my Father!" slumbers deep a "Here,
    my child."

Translation: JAMES FREEMAN CLARKE.

OUR FINEST HOPE.

THE faith that life on earth is being shaped
    To glorious ends ; that order, justice, love,
Mean man's completeness, mean effect as sure
As roundness in the dewdrop, — that great faith
Is but the rushing and expanding stream
Of thought, of feeling, fed by all the past.
Our finest hope is finest memory.

GEORGE ELIOT.

GLIMPSES.

AS one who in the hush of twilight hears
    The pausing pulse of Nature, when the Light
Commingles in the dim, mysterious rite
Of Darkness with the mutual pledge of tears,
Till soft, anon, one timorous star appears,
    Pale-budding as the earliest blossom white
    That comes in Winter's livery bedight,
To hide the gifts of genial Spring she bears, —

So unto me — what time the mysteries
    Of consciousness and slumber weave a dream,
        And pause above it with abated breath,
Like intervals in music — lights arise,
    Beyond prophetic Nature's farthest gleam,
        That teach me half the mystery of Death.

JOHN B. TABB.

"I VEX ME NOT WITH BROODING ON THE YEARS."

I VEX me not with brooding on the years
    That were ere I drew breath; why should I then
Distrust the darkness that may fall again
When life is done? Perchance in other spheres —
Dead planets — I once tasted mortal tears,
    And walked as now among a throng of men,
    Pondering things that lay beyond my ken,
    Questioning death, and solacing my fears.
Ofttimes, indeed, strange sense have I of this, —
    Vague memories that hold me with a spell,
    Touches of unseen lips upon my brow,
Breathing some incommunicable bliss!
    In years foregone, O Soul, was all not well?
    Still lovelier life awaits thee. Fear not thou!

                 THOMAS BAILEY ALDRICH.

A MORNING THOUGHT.

WHAT if some morning, when the stars were
       paling,
    And the dawn whitened, and the east was clear,
Strange peace and rest fell on me from the presence
    Of a benignant Spirit standing near;

And I should tell him, as he stood beside me,
    "This is our Earth, — most friendly Earth and fair;
Daily its sea and shore through sun and shadow
    Faithful it turns, robed in its azure air:

" There is blest living here, loving and serving,
    And quest of truth, and serene friendships dear;
But stay not, Spirit! Earth has one destroyer, —
    His name is Death; flee, lest he find thee here!"

And what if then, while the still morning brightened,
    And freshened in the elm the Summer's breath,
Should gravely smile on me the gentle angel,
    And take my hand and say, "My name is Death!"

                 EDWARD ROWLAND SILL.

THE SOUL'S WASTE.

COULDST thou but keep each noble thought
    Thou fling'st in words away,
With quiet then thy night were fraught,
    With glory crowned thy day.
But thou too idly and too long
    From bower to bower hast ranged;
And Nature trifled with, not loved,
    Will be at last avenged.

With pleasure oft, but ne'er with awe,
    Thou gazest at the skies,
And from thy lips all zephyrs draw
    Their amplest harmonies.
Beware! the hour is coming fast
    When every warbled tone
That brims our hearts with joy shall yield
    No sweetness to thine own.

                 AUBREY DE VERE.

DEFEAT.

I KNEW a captain girded by the foe
    Who might, had not his courage weakly failed,
  Have splendidly the hostile front assailed,
And followed up his vantage blow on blow
Until it reeled and broke and fled.   But no!
  He still must wait until his trumpets hailed
  A hireling troop to help him; then prevailed;
And thought himself a victor doing so.

E'en such an one is he who, sore beset,
  Might conquer by his force of heavenly will;
  But he, poor fool, must wait and wait until
With him vile circumstance has basely met
  To help him through.   Him let no plaudits greet,
  Self conquered with immeasurable defeat.

                              JOHN WHITE CHADWICK.

THE UNPARDONABLE SIN.

IF I have sinned in act, I may repent;
    If I have erred in thought, I may disclaim
My silent error, and yet feel no shame;
But if my soul, big with an ill intent,
Guilty in will, by fate be innocent,
Or being bad yet murmurs at the curse
And incapacity of being worse,
That makes my hungry passion still keep Lent

In keen expectance of a carnival, —
Where in all worlds that round the sun revolve,
And shed their influence on this passive ball,
Abides a power that can my soul absolve?
Could any sin survive and be forgiven, —
One sinful wish would make a hell of heaven.

HARTLEY COLERIDGE.

RARE MOMENTS.

THERE come rare moments when we stir
   Some life-thought into living,
Some feeling stumble on, as 't were,
   That gifts us beyond giving;

When our dull eyes are opened wide
   To life's surrounding glory,
And our deaf ears no longer hide
   Love's all-abounding story;

The soul hath pulses swift and strong
   To sweep this creeping being
Up in the soaring flight of song
   Into immortal seeing;

When we behold ourselves once more
   In spotless strength and beauty,
See straight unto the farther shore
   The paths of truth and duty;

When in the heart the swelling strength
   And bounding hope of nature
Lift man above himself at length,
   A God in soul and stature;

When what is done we see, and what
   Is missed, what now remaining,
And bend our will to work, sink not
   In motionless complaining.

We are again the bright-souled boy,
   With all the world near neighbor;
We feel again the long-lost joy
   Of loving, growing labor.

Hope, faith, and freedom, in one high,
   Triumphant song combining,
Lay bare the secrets of the sky,
   God's providence divining.

The clouds of doubt are torn apart,
   Gone fear with features double,
And, hushed, we beat in God's deep heart,
   Cleansed, healed from grief and trouble.

How small our crawling cares, how slight
   The self-made ills before us!
They were but noises of the night;
   Light now and life restore us.

We are no more earth's broken slave ;
  We reach above our sorrow ;
Joy ! joy ! God gives, as once he gave,
  Again a cloudless morrow.

MERLE ST. CROIX WRIGHT.

SCIENCE.

DAY by day for her darlings
    To her much she added more;
In her hundred-gated Thebes
    Every chamber is a door, —
A door to something grander,
    Loftier walls and vaster floor.

RALPH WALDO EMERSON.

THE TIDE OF FAITH.

SO faith is strong
    Only when we are strong, shrinks when we shrink.
It comes when music stirs us, and the chords,
Moving on some grand climax, shake our souls
With influx new that makes new energies.
It comes in swellings of the heart and tears
That rise at noble and at gentle deeds.
It comes in moments of heroic love,
Unjealous joy in joy not made for us ;
In conscious triumph of the good within,
Making us worship goodness that rebukes.

Even our failures are a prophecy,
Even our yearnings and our bitter tears
After that fair and true we cannot grasp.
Presentiment of better things on earth
Sweeps in with every force that stirs our souls
To admiration, self-renouncing love.

GEORGE ELIOT.

URBS FORTITUDINIS.

OUT of the night that covers me,
    Black as the pit from pole to pole,
I thank whatever gods may be
    For my unconquerable soul.

In the fell clutch of circumstance
    I have not winced nor cried aloud;
Under the bludgeonings of chance
    My head is bloody, but unbowed.

Beyond this place of wrath and tears
    Looms but the horror of the shade,
And yet the menace of the years
    Finds and shall find me unafraid.

It matters not how strait the gate,
    How charged with punishments the scroll,
I am the master of my fate,
    I am the captain of my soul.

WILLIAM E. HENLEY.

AN EGYPTIAN BANQUET.

A CROWDED life, where joy perennial starts;
 The boy's pulse beating 'mid experience sage;
 Wild thirst for action time could ne'er assuage;
Countless sad secrets learned from weary hearts;
New thresholds gained as each full hour departs;
 Long years read singly, each an opened page;
 Love's blissful dreams and friendship's priceless
   gage;
A name grown famous through the streets and marts;
 Knowledge advancing; thoughts that climb and
   climb;
Aims that expand; new pinions that unfurl;
 Age that outstrips all promise of its prime;
Hopes which their prayers at utmost heaven hurl, —
 Till in an instant, in a point of time,
Death, the Egyptian, melts and drinks the pearl.

Thomas Wentworth Higginson.

THE PRICELESS PEARL.

" DEATH, the Egyptian, melts and drinks the
   pearl : "
 And straight a rapture through his being runs,
 A fire that seems the essence of all suns
That ever made the summer's pomp unfurl
Its banners, and the green leaves softly curl

Back from the fruit; a sense of shining ones
   Engirdling round, until his vision shuns
The awful splendor of that radiant whorl.
And then a voice: These things wouldst thou explore?
   Who drinks the pearl of life compounded so
Of love, and joy, and hope, and peace, and pain, —
   All sweetest, saddest things that mortals know, —
Drinks to his own salvation; he shall gain
Life beyond life, and Death shall be no more.

JOHN WHITE CHADWICK.

WHEN HALF-GODS GO.

THE gods man makes he breaks; proclaims them each
   Immortal, and himself outlives them all:
But whom he set not up he cannot reach
   To shake His cloud-dark, sun-bright pedestal.

WILLIAM WATSON.

NON SINE DOLORE.

A SELECTION.

NO passing burden is our earthly sorrow,
   That shall depart in some mysterious morrow.
'T is his one universe where'er we are, —
One changeless law from sun to viewless star.

Were sorrow evil here, evil it were forever,
Beyond the scope and help of our most keen endeavor.
  God doth not dote,
His everlasting purpose shall not fail.
Here where our ears are weary with the wail
And weeping of the sufferers ; there where the Pleiads
          float, —
Here, there, forever, pain most dread and dire
Doth bring the intensest bliss, the dearest and most
          sure.
'T is not from Life aside ; it doth endure
Deep in the secret heart of all existence ;
It is the inward fire,
The heavenly urge and the divine insistence.
  Uplift thine eyes, O Questioner, from the sod !
It were no longer Life,
If ended were the strife ;
Man were not man, God were not truly God.

                    RICHARD WATSON GILDER.

EASTER HYMN.

A S, when the snow still on the bough is clinging,
      And winter will not yet let go her hold,
Sudden we hear a bird returning singing,
      And spring is come to chase away the cold ;

As, when — the clouds beneath the sun disparting —
      The million voices of the sod arise,
Into love's semblance and life's stature starting,
      And lift their anthems to the bending skies, —

MOSES.

From the statue by Michael Angelo.

So may we, Father, through this time of waiting,
    Our spirits for thy coming have prepared,
That every aim unto our life relating
    Shall find fruition in thy will declared.

Lift us and light us on our way, that, casting
    Each burden, doubt, and fear before thy feet,
We may go on in progress everlasting
    Into communion perfect and complete.

And then, what though the winter's pall be o'er us,
    What though the icy touch of death be near, —
The gate of life lies open there before us,
    And thou, O God, in all thy love art here.

               MERLE ST. CROIX WRIGHT.

THE NEW SINAI.

IS there no prophet-soul the while
    To dare, sublimely meek,
Within the shroud of blackest cloud
    The Deity to seek?
'Midst atheistic systems dark,
    And darker hearts' despair,
That soul has heard perchance His word,
    And on the dusky air
His skirts, as passed He by, to see
    Hath strained on their behalf,
Who on the plain, with dance amain,
    Adore the Golden Calf.

'T is but the cloudy darkness dense;
  Though blank the tale it tells,
No God, no Truth! yet He, in sooth,
  Is there — within it dwells:
Within the sceptic darkness deep
  He dwells, that none may see,
Till idol forms and idol thoughts
  Have passed and ceased to be.
No God, no Truth! ah, though in sooth
  So stand the doctrine's half,
On Egypt's track return not back,
  Nor own the Golden Calf!

Take better part, with manlier heart,
  Thine adult spirit can;
No God, no Truth, — receive it ne'er,
  Believe it ne'er, O man!
But turn not then to seek again
  What first the ill began.
No God, it saith; ah, wait in faith
  God's self-completing plan!
Receive it not, but leave it not,
  And wait it out, O man!

" The man that went the cloud within
  Is gone and vanished quite;
He cometh not," the people cries,
  "Nor bringeth God to sight."
" Lo, these thy gods, that safety give;
  Adore, and keep the feast! "

Deluding and deluded cries
 The prophet's brother-priest;
And Israel all bows down to fall
 Before the gilded beast.

Devout indeed! that priestly creed,
 O man, reject as sin;
The clouded hill attend thou still,
 And him that went within.
He yet shall bring some worthy thing
 For waiting souls to see:
Some sacred word that he hath heard
 Their light and life shall be;
Some lofty part, than which the heart
 Adopt no nobler can,
Thou shalt receive, thou shalt believe,
 And thou shalt do, O man!

ARTHUR HUGH CLOUGH.

SHARED.

I SAID it in the meadow path,
 I say it on the mountain stairs,—
The best things any mortal hath
 Are those which every mortal shares.

The air we breathe, the sky, the breeze,
 The light without us and within,—
Life, with its unlocked treasuries,
 God's riches,—are for all to win.

The grass is softer to my tread
  For rest it yields unnumbered feet;
Sweeter to me the wild rose red
  Because she makes the whole world sweet.

Into your heavenly loneliness
  Ye welcomed me, O solemn peaks!
And me in every guest you bless
  Who reverently your mystery seeks.

And, up the radiant peopled way
  That opens into worlds unknown,
It will be life's delight to say,
  "Heaven is not heaven for me alone."

Rich through my brethren's poverty, —
  Such wealth were hideous!   I am blest
Only in what they share with me,
  In what I share with all the rest.

LUCY LARCOM.

MORALITY.

WE cannot kindle when we will
  The fire which in the heart resides;
The spirit bloweth and is still;
  In mystery our soul abides.
    But tasks in hours of insight willed
    Can be through hours of gloom fulfilled.

With aching hands and bleeding feet
　We dig and heap, lay stone on stone;
We bear the burden and the heat
　Of the long day, and wish 't were done.
　　Not till the hours of light return
　　All we have built do we discern.

MATTHEW ARNOLD.

OUR FATHER.

IT were a blessed faith to think
　That God, the great and good,
Had once enshrined himself in man,
　And on his fair earth stood;

Had visited his children here,
　And with a brother's voice,
Hiding his father-tone, had bid
　The world in him rejoice;

Had taught us that we need not shun,
　With heart or lip, to say,
"Our Father" to the One unseen
　Who fills the night and day;

And that our hope man does not die
　Is but the shadow far
Of faith too vast to see direct,
　So deep in it we are.

A blessed faith! and men by it
　　The opened heavens have seen,
And known *God is*, who always else
　　Blind wanderers had been.

And yet if I to win this faith
　　Must own the common earth
Is bare of its Creator's form;
　　That he who gave it birth

Did leave no sign *in me* that I
　　Was born of him, nor spoke
His words of cheer for children now,
　　His silence no more broke, —

Then keep that faith, O God, and give
　　To me, thy yearning one,
The other, greater bond, to be
　　Here, now, thy very son!

And dim that little hope, but teach
　　The one embracing trust,
That what is good God does, and says, —
　　God's self says, — "This I must."

And then I want no other sign;
　　Reveal thyself no more;
That human semblance orphans me,
　　Seen, but so long before.

"MY CHILD IS LYING ON MY KNEES."

From the painting, "Mother's Joy," by Oscar Begas.

And if to me to live seem good,
　　Thy goodness conquers mine;
Or should not life, but death, await,
　　My choice I glad resign,

Sure still that there is higher good,
　　That life is not my gain,
That what I think is happiness
　　Thou knowest would be pain.

WILLIAM C. GANNETT.

HYMN FOR THE MOTHER.

MY child is lying on my knees;
　　The signs of heaven she reads;
My face is all the heaven she sees,
　　Is all the heaven she needs.

And she is well, yea, bathed in bliss,
　　If heaven is in my face;
Behind it is all tenderness
　　And truthfulness and grace.

I mean her well so earnestly,
　　Unchanged in changing mood,
My life would go without a sigh
　　To bring her something good.

I also am a child, and I
　　Am ignorant and weak;
I gaze upon the starry sky,
　　And then I must not speak;

For all behind the starry sky,
　　Behind the world so broad,
Behind men's hearts and souls doth lie
　　The infinite of God.

If true to her, though troubled sore,
　　I cannot choose but be,
Thou, who art peace forevermore,
　　Art very true to me.

If I am low and sinful, bring
　　More love where need is rife;
Thou knowest what an awful thing
　　It is to be a life.

Hast thou not wisdom to enwrap
　　My waywardness about,
In doubting safety on the lap
　　Of Love that knows no doubt?

Lo! Lord, I sit in thy wide space,
　　My child upon my knee;
She looketh up unto my face,
　　And I look up to thee.

GEORGE MACDONALD.

AT ANCHOR.

HOW calm upon the twilight water sleeps,
  With folded wings, yon solitary sail,
Safe-harbored, haply dreaming of the gale
That wolf-like o'er the waste deserted leaps!
One star — a signal light above her — keeps
  Watch; and, behold, its pictured image pale
  Gleams far below, a seeming anchor frail,
Where onward still the noiseless current sweeps!

Star of my life, pale planet, far removed,
  Oh, be thou, when the twilight deepens, near!
Set in my soul thine image undisproved
  By death and darkness, till the morning clear
Behold me in the presence I have loved,
  My beacon here, my bliss eternal there!

JOHN B. TABB.

NO UNBELIEF.

THERE is no unbelief;
  Whoever plants a leaf beneath the sod,
And waits to see it push away the clod,
  Trusts he in God.

Whoever says, when clouds are in the sky,
"Be patient, heart! light breaketh by and by,"
  Trusts the Most High.

Whoever sees 'neath winter's field of snow
The silent harvest of the future grow,
 God's power must know.

Whoever lies down on his couch to sleep,
Content to lock each sense in slumber deep,
 Knows God will keep.

Whoever says, " To-morrow," " The unknown,"
" The future," trusts that Power alone
 He dares disown.

The heart that looks on when the eyelids close,
And dares to live when life has only woes,
 God's comfort knows.

 There is no unbelief;
And day by day, and night, unconsciously,
The heart lives by that faith the lips deny;
 God knoweth why.

LIZZIE YORK CASE.

THE MARCHING MORROWS.

NOW gird thee well for courage,
 My knight of twenty year,
Against the marching morrows,
That fill the world with fear.

The flowers fade before them;
The summer leaves the hill;
Their trumpets range the morning,
And those who hear grow still.

Like pillagers of harvest,
Their fame is far abroad,
As gray, remorseless troopers,
That plunder and maraud.

The dust is on their corselets;
Their marching fills the world;
With conquest after conquest
Their banners are unfurled.

They overthrow the battles
Of every lord of war,
From world-dominioned cities
Wipe out the names they bore.

Sohrab, Rameses, Roland,
Ramoth, Napoleon, Tyre,
And the Romeward Huns of Attila, —
Alas, for their desire!

By April and by autumn
They perish in their pride,
And still they close and gather
Out of the mountain-side.

The tanned and tameless children
Of the wild elder earth,
With stature of the northlights,
They have the stars for girth.

There 's not a hand to stay them
Of all the hearts that brave,
No captain to undo them,
No cunning to off-stave.

Yet fear thou not!   If haply
Thou be the kingly one,
They 'll set thee in their vanguard
To lead them round the sun.

BLISS CARMAN.

WELL SATISFIED.

From " The Sick Stock-Rider."

I 'VE had my share of pastime, and I 've done my
        share of toil ;
    And life is short, — the longest life a span.
I care not now to tarry for the corn or for the oil,
    Or for the wine that maketh glad the heart of man.
For good undone and gifts misspent and resolutions
        vain,
    'T is somewhat late to trouble.   This I know, —
I should live the same life over, if I had to live again ;
    And the chances are I go where most men go.

The deep blue skies wax dusky, and the tall green
        trees grow dim ;
    The sward beneath me seems to heave and fall ;
And sickly, smoky shadows through the sleepy sun-
        light swim,

And on the very sun's face weave their pall.
Let me slumber in the hollow where the wattle-blossoms
wave,
With never stone or rail to fence my bed.
Should the sturdy station-children pull the bush-
flowers on my grave,
I may chance to hear them romping overhead.

A. Lindsay Gordon.

THE TOUCHSTONE.

A MAN there came, whence none can tell,
  Bearing a touchstone in his hand,
And tested all things in the land
By its unerring spell.

A thousand transformations rose
From fair to foul, from foul to fair;
The golden crown he did not spare,
Nor scorn the beggar's clothes.

Of heirloom jewels, prized so much,
Were many changed to chips and clods;
And even statues of the gods
Crumbled beneath its touch.

Then angrily the people cried:
"The loss outweighs the profit far.
Our goods suffice us as they are;
We will not have them tried."

And, since they could not so avail
To check his unrelenting quest,
They seized him, saying, " Let him test
How real is our jail."

But though they slew him with the sword,
And in a fire his touchstone burned,
Its doings could not be o'erturned,
Its undoings restored.

And when, to stop all future harm,
They strewed its ashes on the breeze,
They little guessed each grain of these
Conveyed the perfect charm.

WILLIAM ALLINGHAM.

DEEP UNTO DEEP.

DEEP calleth unto deep!
   Tossed on a stormy sea,
I heard a strong voice calling out,
  " What drift is bearing me?
Is it to haven? out to main?
To rest, to toil? to loss, to gain?"

Across the doubtful tide
  Rang out the answer grand:
" I see a blue sky overhead,
  Although I see no land;
So breast the surges, bear the doubt,
And search the blue sky's meaning out."

Serene and still and strong,
 Though good or ill betide,
Bends the great mystery of hope,
 Love's prophet, reason's guide.
What must it mean? It wraps us round,
And saves us, though the tempests sound.

Safe on this higher sea
 We trust life's dearest freight;
Immortal tides of deathless thought
 Sweep onward while we wait;
And love's strong voices, o'er and o'er,
Shout promise of another shore.

MRS. W. J. POTTER.

COURAGE.

BECAUSE I hold it sinful to despond,
 And will not let the bitterness of life
Blind me with burning tears, but look beyond
 Its tumult and its strife;

Because I lift my head above the mist,
 Where the sun shines and the broad breezes blow,
By every ray and every raindrop kissed
 That God's love doth bestow, —

Think you I find no bitterness at all,
 No burden to be borne like Christian's pack?
Think you there are no ready tears to fall
 Because I keep them back?

Why should I hug life's ills with cold reserve
   To curse myself and all who love me? Nay,
A thousand times more good than I deserve
   God gives me every day.

And in each one of these rebellious tears,
   Kept bravely back, he makes a rainbow shine.
Grateful, I take his slightest gift; no fears,
   Nor any doubts are mine.

Dark skies must clear; and when the clouds are past,
   One golden day redeems the weary year.
Patient, I listen, sure that sweet at last
   Will sound his voice of cheer.

Then vex me not with chiding. Let me be.
   I must be glad and grateful to the end.
I grudge you not your cold and darkness, — me
   The powers of light befriend.

CELIA THAXTER.

OUT OF CHILDHOOD.

> But thou and I are one in kind,
>   As moulded like in Nature's mint;
>   And hill and wood and field did print
> The same sweet forms in either mind.
>
> "*In Memoriam.*"

THERE was a stream, low-voiced and shy;
   So narrow was the lazy tide,
  The reeds that grew on either side
Crossed their green swords against the sky.

And in the stream a shallow boat,
  With prow thrust deep among the reeds,
  And broad stern wound with water-weeds,
Lay half aground and half afloat.

And in the boat, hand clasping hand,
  Two children sat as in a dream,
  Their eyes upon the lapsing stream,
Their faces turned away from land.

They cared not for a little rift
  That came between them and the shore,
  And softly widened more and more
Till on the stream they lay adrift.

They murmured absently and low
  That presently they must return
  To their sweet store of gathered fern
And tinted pebbles ranged in row.

Through limpid pools they drifted slow;
  They looked before and not behind,
  And fancied still they heard the wind
That through the weeds went whispering low.

The lengthening ripples wore a crest,
  The white foam grew beneath the stern,
  And, murmuring still, "We will return,"
The river bore them on its breast.

They hailed the homeward-flitting bee,
  They smelled the rose upon the shore,
  The current widened more and more,
The river bore them to the sea.

Now over ocean caves impearled
  Unheedingly they drift and drift,
  And know not that the little rift
Has widened into half the world.

And like the pearls in ocean caves
  The vision of their lost delight
  Is whelmed and flooded out of sight
By thoughts on thoughts, like waves on waves.

And would they — what they never will,
  And could they — what they never can,
  Turn back through space as 't were a span,
And stand again beside the rill,

Its shallow rhythm, as it glides
  Through tangled sedge and feathery ferns,
  Would vex the wakening sense that learns
The chant of winds, the sweep of tides.

Yet sometimes, when the wind is low,
  And sunken treasure of the caves
  Shines faintly upward through the waves,
The old thought rises even so.

And while they watch, as in a dream,
  The circling drift of ocean-weeds,
  They babble still of those green reeds
That crossed their swords above the stream.

                    HELEN THAYER HUTCHESON.

PROTECTING SHADOWS.

I SIT beneath the elm's protecting shadow,
  Whose graceful form
  Shelters from sunshine warm;
While far around me, in the heated meadow,
  The busy insects swarm.
Better than any roof, these softly swaying leaves,
Opening and closing to the passing air,
Which from afar the fragrant breath receives
  Of forest odors rare.
   And, as the branches sway,
Revealing depths on depths of heavenly blue,
The tempered rays of sunshine, glancing through
In flickering spots of light, around me play;
While little birds dart through the mazy web,
  With happy chirp and song,
  Fearing no wrong,
To their half-hidden nests above my head.
Thus, without motion, without speech or sound,
I rest, a part of all this life around.

Beneath the shadow of the Great Protection
  The soul sits, hushed and calm.
Bathed in the peace of that divine affection,
No fever-heats of life or dull dejection
  Can work the spirit harm.
  Diviner heavens above
  Look down on it in love.

And, as the varying winds move where they will,
In whispers soft, through trackless fields of air,
So comes the Spirit's breath, serene and still,
Its tender messages of love to bear
From men of every race and speech and zone,
    Making the whole world one,
Till every sword shall to a sickle bend,
And the long, weary strifes of earth shall end.

    Be happy, then, my heart,
      That thou in all hast part, —
In all these outward gifts of time and sense;
In all the spirit's nobler influence;
    In sun and snow and storm;
In the vast life which flows through sea and sky,
Through every changing form
Whose beauty soon must die;
In the things seen, which ever pass away;
In things unseen, which shall forever stay;
    In the Eternal Love
    That lifts the soul above
All earthly passion, grief, remorse, and care,
    Which lower life must bear.
    Be happy now and ever,
Since from the Love divine no power the soul shall
      sever:
    For not our feeble nor our stormy past,
    Nor shadows from the future backward cast;
Not all the gulfs of evil far below,
Nor mountain-peaks of good which soar on high
    Into the unstained sky,

Nor any power the universe can know;
Not the vast laws to whose control is given
The blades of grass just springing from the sod,
And stars within the unsounded depths of heaven,
Can touch the spirit hid with Christ in God:
For nought that he has made, below, above,
  Can part us from his love.

     JAMES FREEMAN CLARKE.

A LONGING.

NOT in lands with a speech not my own,
 Where the sights that are newest look lone,
But where all most familiar had grown
To my eyes and the throbs of my breast, —
  Shall I die in my nest?

They will say, It is one to the wise
From what country the freed spirit flies,
For the way is the same to the skies:
Truths to faith and to reason addressed, —
  But alas! for the nest.

Oh, methinks it would glad the last gaze
To be circled with friends of old days,
And the spots that are gilt with the rays
That stream from the sun of the west
  O'er the down of my nest!

    Translation: N. L. FROTHINGHAM.

FREEDOM OF THE MIND.

HIGH walls and huge the *body* may confine,
   And iron grates obstruct the prisoner's gaze,
And massive bolts may baffle his design,
And vigilant keepers watch his devious ways;
Yet scorns the immortal *mind* this base control!
No chains can bind it, and no cell enclose.
Swifter than light, it flies from pole to pole,
And in a flash from earth to heaven it goes!
It leaps from mount to mount; from vale to vale
It wanders, plucking honeyed fruits and flowers;
It visits home, to hear the fireside tale,
Or in sweet converse pass the joyous hours.
'T is up before the sun, roaming afar,
And in its watches wearies every star!

WILLIAM LLOYD GARRISON

IMMORTALITY.

FOILED by our fellow-men, depressed, outworn,
   We leave the brutal world to take its way;
And, *Patience! in another life*, we say,
The world shall be thrust down, and we upborne.

And will not, then, the immortal armies scorn
The world's poor routed leavings? or will they,
Who failed under the heat of this life's day,
Support the fervors of the heavenly morn?

No, no! the energy of life may be
Kept on after the grave, but not begun;
And he who flagged not in the earthly strife,

From strength to strength advancing, — only he,
His soul well knit, and all his battles won,
Mounts, and that hardly, to eternal life.

MATTHEW ARNOLD.

IRREVOCABLE.

WHAT thou hast done thou hast done; for the
heavenly horses are swift.
Think not their flight to o'ertake, — they stand at the
throne even now.
Ere thou canst compass the thought, the immortals in
just hands shall lift,
Poise, and weigh surely thy deed, and its weight shall
be laid on thy brow;
For what thou hast done thou hast done.

What thou hast not done remains; and the heavenly
horses are kind.
Till thou hast pondered thy choice, they will patiently
wait at thy door.
Do a brave deed, and behold! they are farther away
than the wind.
Returning, they bring thee a crown, to shine on thy
brow evermore;
For what thou hast done thou hast done.

MARY WRIGHT PLUMMER.

HIDE NOT THY HEART.

THIS is my creed,
    This be my deed, —
" Hide not thy heart ! "
Soon we depart ;
Mortals are all ;
A breath, then the pall ;
A flash on the dark —
All 's done — stiff and stark.
No time for a lie ;
The truth, and then die.
Hide not thy heart !

Forth with thy thought !
Soon 't will be nought,
And thou in thy tomb.
Now is air, now is room.
Down with false shame ;
Reck not of fame ;
Dread not man's spite ;
Quench not thy light.
This be thy creed,
This be thy deed, —
" Hide not thy heart ! "

If God is, he made
Sunshine and shade,
Heaven and hell ;
This we know well.
Dost thou believe ?

Do not deceive;
Scorn not thy faith, —
If 't is a wraith,
Soon it will fly.
Thou, who must die,
Hide not thy heart!

This is my creed,
This be my deed:
Faith or a doubt,
I shall speak out,
And hide not my heart.

RICHARD WATSON GILDER.

FROM THE ETERNAL SHADOW.

FROM the eternal shadow, rounding
    All our sun and starlight here,
Voices of our loved ones sounding
    Bid us be of heart and cheer,
Through the silence, down the spaces,
    Falling on the inward ear.

Let us draw their mantles o'er us
    Which have fallen on our way;
Let us do the work before us,
    Bravely, cheerly, while we may,
Ere the long night-silence cometh,
    And with us it is not day.

JOHN GREENLEAF WHITTIER.

LOVE AND DEATH.

WHEN the end comes, and we must say good-by,
    And I am going to the quiet land;
And, sitting in some loved place hand in hand,
For the last time together, you and I,
We watch the winds blow, and the sunlight lie
    Soft by the washing of the western foam,
    Above the spaces of our garden home,
Where we have lived and loved in days passed by, —
We must not weep, my darling, or upbraid
    The quiet death who comes to part us twain,
    But know that parting would not be such pain
Had not our love a perfect flower been made.
And we shall find it in God's garden laid
    On that sweet day wherein we meet again.

ANONYMOUS.

THE RIDDLE OF THE SPHINX.

O LIFE, I hold thee face to face;
    Nor move I back one single pace
For accident of time or space.

For time and space to me belong,
Nor know they how to work me wrong.
I wait; for I, not thou, am strong.

Day after day may slow go by;
After the worst that thou canst try,
At last, at last, thou shalt reply!

THE RIDDLE OF THE SPHINX.

From a photograph.

No haste, — Eternity is now;
No rest, — I will not let thee go;
What thou hast asked, that answer thou!

ANNA C. BRACKETT.

THE INDWELLING GOD.

HE is the green in every blade,
   The health in every boy and maid;
In yonder sunrise flag he blooms
Above a nation's well-earned tombs;
That empty sleeve his arm contains,
That blushing scar his life-blood drains;
That flaunting cheek against the lamp
He hoists for succor from a heart
Where love maintains its wasted camp
Till love arrive to take its part;
That bloodless cheek against the pane
Goes whitening all the murky street
With God's own dread, lest hunger gain
Upon his love's woe-burdened feet.

JOHN WEISS.

NATURA NATURANS.

NATURE is made better by no mean
   But nature makes that mean: even that art
Which you say adds to nature is an art
That nature makes.

WILLIAM SHAKSPERE.

COSMIC EMOTION.

THY voice is on the rolling air;
    I hear thee where the waters run;
    Thou standest in the rising sun,
And in the setting thou art fair.

What art thou, then? I cannot guess;
    But though I seem in sun and flower
    To feel thee some diffusive power,
I do not therefore love thee less.

Far off thou art, but ever nigh;
    I have thee still, and I rejoice;
    I prosper, circled by thy voice;
I shall not lose thee, though I die.

ALFRED TENNYSON.

THE BLINDING LIGHT.

MYSTERIOUS Night! when our first parent
        knew
    Thee from report divine, and heard thy name,
    Did he not tremble for this lovely frame,
This glorious canopy of light and blue?
Yet, 'neath a curtain of translucent dew,
    Bathed in the rays of the great setting flame,
    Hesperus, with the host of heaven, came,
And lo! Creation widened in man's view.

Who could have thought such darkness lay concealed
    Within thy beams, O Sun! or who could find,
Whilst fly and leaf and insect stood revealed,
    That to such countless orbs thou mad'st us blind?
Why do we then shun death with anxious strife?
If Light can thus deceive, wherefore not Life?

                  JOSEPH BLANCO WHITE.

THROUGH GREAT TRIBULATION.

THERE must be refuge! Men
    Perished in winter winds till one smote fire
From flint-stones coldly hiding what they held, —
The red spark treasured from the kindling sun;
They gorged on flesh like wolves till one sowed corn,
Which grew a weed, yet makes the life of man;
They mowed and babbled till some tongue struck
        speech,
And patient fingers framed the lettered sound.
What good gift have my brothers, but it came
From search and strife and loving sacrifice?

                  EDWIN ARNOLD.

THE COMING MAN.

MAN'S self is not yet man.
    Nor shall I deem his object served, his end
Attained, his genuine strength put fairly forth,
While only here and there a star dispels

The darkness, here and there a towering mind
O'erlooks its prostrate fellows.   When the host
Is out at once, to the despair of night;
When all mankind alike is perfected,
Equal in full-blown powers, — then, not till then,
I say, begins man's general infancy.

ROBERT BROWNING.

EVENING.

A THOUGHTFUL life is a pleasant life, —
   Yea, dreams in a wild-brier lane;
The air soft kindling, with the moon
   Midway of her stately reign,

Where the broad light lies wavelessly,
   Where the toiling sun has lain,
A tree and its shadow, wondrous still,
   Ruling the grassy plain.

The river to the distant sea,
   Murmuring, murmuring, goes,
Type of a life that broods and sings
   On to its quiet close.

Thanks, that along the shifting sands,
   As moves our sleepless tent,
Moments of higher calm are given,
   And of more true content!

EVENING.

From the painting by C. Bernier.

Content, — the world falls off, and leaves
  A measure nobler grained,
By which I try the seeming lost,
  As well as seeming gained.

Dear heart, whose pulses with my own
  Keep their mysterious move,
That fillest every transient pause
  With music of thy love,

Art not thou patient too to-night,
  Divining what true strength,
What life is ours, what joy to come,
  And far-off calm at length?

ANNE WHITNEY.

THE KINGS.

A MAN said unto his angel:
  My spirits are fallen thro',
And I cannot carry this battle.
O brother! what shall I do?

The terrible kings are on me,
  With spears that are deadly bright;
Against me so from the cradle
  Do fate and my fathers fight.

Then said to the man his angel:
  Thou wavering, foolish soul,
Back to the ranks! What matter,
  To win or to lose the whole,

As judged by the little judges
Who hearken not well, nor see?
Not thus, by the outer issue,
The wise shall interpret thee.

Thy will is the very, the only,
The solemn event of things;
The weakest of hearts defying
Is stronger than all these kings.

Tho' out of the past they gather,
Mind's Doubt and Bodily Pain,
And pallid Thirst of the Spirit,
That is kin to the other twain,

And Grief, in a cloud of banners,
And ringleted Vain Desires,
And Vice, with the spoils upon him
Of thee and thy beaten sires,

While kings of eternal evil
Yet darken the hills about, —
Thy part is, with broken sabre,
To rise on the last redoubt;

To fear not sensible failure,
Nor covet the game at all,
But fighting, fighting, fighting,
Die, driven against the wall!

LOUISE IMOGEN GUINEY.

IN HOC SIGNO.

A ND if his church be doubtful, it is sure
  That in a world, made for whatever else,
Not made for mere enjoyment; in a world
Of toil but half requited, or, at best,
Paid in some futile currency of breath;
A world of incompleteness, sorrow swift,
And consolation laggard, — whatsoe'er
The form of building or the creed professed,
The cross, bold type of shame to homage turned,
Of an unfinished life that sways the world,
Shall tower as sovereign emblem over all.

       JAMES RUSSELL LOWELL.

SADNESS AND GLADNESS.

T HERE was a glory in my house,
  And it is fled;
There was a baby at my heart,
  And it is dead.

And when I sit and think of him,
  I am so sad
That half it seems that never more
  Can I be glad.

If you had known this baby mine,
  He was so sweet,
You would have gone a journey just
  To kiss his feet.

He could not walk a single step,
    Nor speak a word;
But then he was as blithe and gay
    As any bird

That ever sat on orchard bough
    And trilled its song
Until the listener fancied it
    As sweet and strong

As if from lips of angels he
    Had heard it flow, —
Such angels as thy hand could paint,
    Angelico!

You cannot think how many things
    He learned to know
Before the swift, swift angel came,
    And bade him go;

So that my neighbors said of him,
    He was so wise
That he was never meant for earth,
    But for the skies.

But I would not believe a word
    Of what they said;
Nor will I, even now, although
    My boy is dead.

For God would be most wicked, if,
    When all the earth
Is in the travail of a new
    And heavenly birth,

As often as a little Christ is found
    With human breath,
He, like another Herod, should resolve
    Upon its death.

But should you ask me how it is
    That yours can stay,
Though mine must spread his little wings
    And fly away,

I could but say that God, who made
    This heart of mine,
Must have intended that its love
    Should be the sign

Of his own love; and that if he
    Can think it right
To turn my joy to sorrow, and
    My day to night,

I cannot doubt that he will turn,
    In other ways,
My winter darkness to the light
    Of summer days.

I know that God gives nothing to
    Us for a day;
That what he gives he never cares
    To take away;

And when he comes and seems to make
    Our glory less,
It is that, by and by, we may
    The more confess

That he has made it brighter than
 It was before, —
A glory shining on and on
 Forevermore.

And when I sit and think of this,
 I am so glad
That half it seems that never more
 Can I be sad.

JOHN WHITE CHADWICK.

THE BABY OVER THE WAY.

THERE is the window over the way
 That was lit with a baby's face by day;
But the shutters are closed, and at the door
The doctor's gig for an hour has stood,
 And they tell us — the little gossips four,
Who bring us the news of the neighborhood —
 That the doctor is coming every day
 To see the baby over the way.

.   .   .   .   .   .

When midnight hushes the city's noise,
We hear the sound of a feeble voice,
 And know that the room where the light burns low
Holds hearts that watch for the morning light.
 What the day shall bring, if they could but know,
They would cling to the lingering hours of night;
 For hearts will break with the breaking day,
 When the long watch closes over the way.

The baby over the way is dead,
And the mourners will not be comforted.
  O desolate ones, no stranger's voice
May break your silence, for words are cheap!
  Your griefs we tell by our tenderest joys:
Our four little gossips are warm asleep.
    Would it lighten your burden if you knew
    That here, in the dark, we were crying with you?

G. WASHINGTON GLADDEN

MY OWN.

BROWN heads and gold around my knee
    Dispute in eager play;
Sweet childish voices in my ear
    Are sounding all the day;
Yet sometimes in a sudden hush
    I seem to hear a tone
Such as my little boy's had been,
    If I had kept my own.

And ofttimes when they come to me,
    As evening hours grow long,
And beg me winningly to give
    A story or a song,
I see a pair of star-bright eyes
    Among the others shine, —
The eyes of him who ne'er hath heard
    Story or song of mine.

At night I go my round, and pause
  Each white-draped cot beside,
And note how flushed is this one's cheek,
  How that one's curls lie wide;
And to a corner tenantless
  My swift thoughts go apace,
That would have been, if he had lived,
  My other darling's place.

The years go fast; my children soon
  Within the world of men
Will find their work, and venture forth,
  Not to return again.
But there is one who cannot go,—
  I shall not be alone:
The little one who did not live
  Will always be my own.

                    MARY WRIGHT PLUMMER.

WILL IT BE THUS?

HOW oft, escaping from some troubled dream,
    With stifled sob and eyelids strangely wet,
We hail with joy the morn's assuring gleam,
  And smile, and quite forget!

Will it be thus when, waking after death,
  The horror fades that we had known erewhile?
When all life's struggle ends in one glad breath,
  Shall we forget, and smile?

                    EMMA HUNTINGTON NASON.

"JOY COMETH WITH THE MORNING."

From the painting, "Morning," by J. Marlak.

UP–HILL.

DOES the road wind up-hill all the way?
  Yes, to the very end.
Will the day's journey take the whole long day?
  From morn to night, my friend.

But is there for the night a resting-place?
  A roof for when the slow, dark hours begin.
May not the darkness hide it from my face?
  You cannot miss that inn.

Shall I meet other wayfarers at night?
  Those who have gone before.
Then must I knock or call when just in sight?
  They will not keep you standing at that door.

Shall I find comfort, travel-sore and weak?
  Of labor you shall find the sum.
Will there be beds for me and all who seek?
  Yes, beds for all who come.

CHRISTINA GEORGINA ROSSETTI.

JOY COMETH WITH THE MORNING.

OUT of the dreams and the dust of ages,
  Hindu reverie, Hebrew boy,
Deeds of heroes, and lore of sages,
  Comes the hope that turns earth to joy.

But the rosy light of the morning teaches
　A blither knowledge than books can tell,
And the song that runs through the orchard preaches
　The ceaseless message that all is well.

Hark to the lesson that Nature meaneth !
　List to the breeze on the pine-clad hill !
See, the sun-rays stream to the zenith !
　Thrice the oriole whistles shrill.

Myriad odors are faint and tender,
　Sweet notes come from the woodlands far ;
Draw fresh life from the day's new splendor,
　Pluck thy hope from the morning star.

THOMAS WENTWORTH HIGGINSON.

ANTICIPATION.

HOW doth Death speak of our beloved,
　　When it has laid them low, —
When it has set its hallowing touch
　On speechless lips and brow ?

It clothes their every gift and grace
With radiance from the holiest place,
With light as from an angel's face.

It sweeps their faults with heavy hand,
As sweeps the sea the trampled sand,
Till scarce the faintest print is scanned.

It takes each failing on our part,
And brands it in upon the heart
With caustic power and cruel art.

Thus doth Death speak of our beloved,
 When it has laid them low;
Then let Love antedate Death's work,
 And do this *now*.
     Mrs. Charles.

CARPE DIEM.

HOW the dull thought smites me dumb, —
 "It will come!" and "It will come!"
But to-day I am not dead;
Life in hand and foot and head
Leads me on its wondrous ways.
'T is in such poor, common days,
Made of morning, noon, and night,
Golden truth has leaped to light,
Potent messages have sped,
Torches flashed with running rays,
World-runes started on their flight.

Let it come, when come it must;
But To-Day from out the dust
Blooms and brightens like a flower,
Fair with love, and faith, and power.
Pluck it with unclouded will,
From the great tree Igdrasil.
    Edward Rowland Sill.

THE TWOFOLD AWE.

Two things fill my mind with awe, — the heavens above me, and
the moral law within. — IMMANUEL KANT.

"TWO things," said he of Königsberg,
   Most gravely wise of modern men,
" With awe my spirit fill whene'er
   They break upon my ken:
The starry heavens, when they show
   Their countless hosts in order bright;
The Law within, which teaches me
   The way of Truth and Right."

How poor the man who cannot say
   Amen to words so sweet and strong,
Whose heart has never known the beat
   Of either mystic song!
Has never felt abashed and stilled
   By starry splendors, cool and far;
Nor, when the inward silence thrilled,
   How weak and strong we are!

But, oh that each might win the grace
   To hold the twofold awe as one,
To blend the inward voice with that
   Which speaks in star and sun;
From shining orbs that never swerve
   Upon their high and glorious way,
The strength attain whereby he might
   That law within obey!

Then would our lives as bravely shine
   As ever pomp of clearest night;
For suns and moons and stars are pale
   To Love and Truth and Right.
And then on who in darkness sit
   Should gladsome light arise and shine;
And in our glory men should walk,
   And conquer by our sign.

JOHN WHITE CHADWICK.

LIFE.

O LIFE! that mystery that no man knows,
   And all men ask: the Arab from his sands;
The Cæsar's self, lifting imperial hands;
And the lone dweller where the lotus blows.
O'er trackless tropics, and o'er silent snows,
She dumbly broods, that Sphinx of all the lands;
And if she answers, no man understands,
And no cry breaks the blank of her repose.
But a new form rose once upon my pain,
With grave, sad lips, but in the eyes a smile
Of deepest meaning dawning sweet and slow,
Lighting to service; and no more in vain
I ask of Life, "What art thou?" as erewhile,
For since Love holds my hand, I seem to know.

LIZZIE M. LITTLE.

HE GIVETH SNOW.

PAIN ushered in the sullen day.
    " Oh, cold, gray day," I said,
" I only asked one little ray
    Of hope, and hope is dead ! "

Like some great brooding bird above,
    The sky let fall its feathery down.
" Take the dark earth," she said, " my love !
    Weave Nature's bridal gown ! "

I opened wide the snowy door;
    The soft flakes fluttered round my head.
" Beauty, at least, lives evermore."
    I turned, but pain had fled.

                MARY THACHER HIGGINSON.

LOVE'S NOBILITY.

FOR this is Love's nobility:
    Not to scatter bread and gold,
Goods and raiment, bought and sold;
But to hold fast our simple sense,
And speak the speech of innocence,
And with hand and body and blood
To make our bosom counsel good.
For he that feeds men serveth few ;
He serves all who dares be true.

                RALPH WALDO EMERSON.

DULCE ET DECORUM.

MANY loved Truth, and lavished life's best oil
    Amid the dust of books to find her,
Content at last for guerdon of their toil
    With the cast mantle she hath left behind her;
    Many in sad faith sought for her;
    Many with crossed hands sighed for her;
But these our brothers fought for her,
At life's dear peril wrought for her,
So loved her that they died for her,
    Tasting the raptured fleetness
    Of her divine completeness:
Their higher instinct knew
Those love her best who to themselves are true,
And what they dare to dream of dare to do.
    They followed her, and found her
Where all may hope to find, —
Not in the ashes of the burnt-out mind,
But beautiful, with danger's sweetness round her,
    Where faith made whole with deed
Breathes its awakening breath
    Into the lifeless creed;
    They saw her plumed and mailed,
    With sweet, stern face unveiled,
And all-repaying eyes look proud on them in death.

JAMES RUSSELL LOWELL.

THE GOOD MOMENTS.

OH, we 're sunk enough here, God knows!
    But not quite so sunk that moments,
Sure, though seldom, are denied us,
    When the spirit's true endowments
Stand out plainly from its false ones,
    And apprise it if pursuing
Or the right way or the wrong way,
    To its triumph or undoing.

There are flashes struck from midnights,
    There are fire-flames noondays kindle,
Whereby piled-up honors perish,
    Whereby swol'n ambitions dwindle;
While just this or that poor impulse,
    Which for once had play unstifled,
Seems the sole work of a lifetime
    That away the rest have trifled.

ROBERT BROWNING.

THE PROMISE OF SPRING.

GOD does not send us strange flowers every year.
    When the spring winds blow o'er the pleasant
        places,
The same dear things lift up the same fair faces;
    The violet is here.

It all comes back, the odor, grace, and hue,
Each sweet relation of its life repeated;
Nothing is lost; no looking-for is cheated;
　　It is the thing we knew.

So after the death-winter it will be:
God will not put strange sights in heavenly places;
The old love will look out from the old faces;
　　VIOLET, I shall have thee.

A. D. T. WHITNEY.

THE SECRET.

SHE passes in her beauty bright
　　Amongst the mean, amongst the gay,
And all are brighter for the sight,
　　And bless her as she goes her way.

And now a gleam of pity pours,
　　And now a spark of spirit flies,
Uncounted, from the unlocked stores
　　Of her rich lips and precious eyes.

And all men look, and all men smile,
　　But no man looks on her as I;
They mark her for a little while,
　　But I will watch her till I die.

And if I wonder now and then
　　Why this so strange a thing should be,
That she be seen by wiser men,
　　And only duly loved by me,

I only wait a little longer,
   And watch her radiance in the room,
Here making light a little stronger,
   And there obliterating gloom

(Like one who in a tangled way
   Watches the broken sun fall through,
Turning to gold the faded spray,
   And making diamonds of dew),

Until at last, as my heart burns,
   She gathers all her scattered light,
And undivided radiance turns
   Upon me like a sea of light;

And then I know they see in part
   That which God lets me worship whole:
He gives them glances of her heart,
   But me the sunshine of her soul.

              Cosmo Monkhouse.

THE BETTER TIME.

OBERMANN LOQUITUR.

DESPAIR not thou as I despaired,
   Nor be cold gloom thy prison!
Forward the gracious hours have fared,
   And, see! the sun is risen.

He melts the icebergs of the past;
   A green, new earth appears;
Millions, whose life in ice lay fast,
   Have thoughts and smiles and tears.

The world's great order dawns in sheen,
   After long darkness rude,
Divinelier imaged, clearer seen,
   With happier goal pursued.

MATTHEW ARNOLD.

WELL PAID.

HEAR how the brooding cushat mourns
   Her love. We will not mourn or weep,
Or lock ourselves in wintry sleep,
But bide in peace Heaven's large returns.
All that he has and is, who gives,
With whom no earth-born wish survives
To hoard his little grief or bliss,
God his great debtor surely is,
And pays infinity. Who meet
The coming fate half-way, and fling
Their blessed treasures at her feet,
Shall feel through all her clamoring,
Her hard eye quail; she knows 't were vain
To empty what God brims again.

ANNE WHITNEY.

ABRAHAM DAVENPORT.

IN the old days (a custom laid aside
    With breeches and cocked hats) the people sent
Their wisest men to make the public laws.
And so, from a brown homestead where the Sound
Drinks the small tribute of the Mianas,
Waved over by the woods of Rippowams,
And hallowed by pure lives and tranquil deaths,
Stamford sent up to the councils of the State
Wisdom and grace in Abraham Davenport.

'T was on a May day of the far old year
Seventeen hundred eighty that there fell
Over the bloom and sweet life of the spring,
Over the fresh earth and the heaven of noon,
A horror of great darkness, like the night
In day of which the Norland sagas tell, —
The Twilight of the Gods.   The low-hung sky
Was black with ominous clouds, save where its rim
Was fringed with a dull glow, like that which climbs
The crater's sides from the red hell below.
Birds ceased to sing, and all the barnyard fowls
Roosted; the cattle at the pasture bars
Lowed and looked homeward; bats on leathern wings
Flitted abroad; the sounds of labor died;
Men prayed, and women wept; all ears grew sharp
To hear the doom-blast of the trumpet shatter

The black sky, that the dreadful face of Christ
Might look from the rent clouds, not as he looked
A loving guest at Bethany, but stern
As Justice and inexorable Law.

Meanwhile in the old State House, dim as ghosts,
Sat the lawgivers of Connecticut,
Trembling beneath their legislative robes.
" It is the Lord's Great Day !   Let us adjourn,"
Some said; and then, as if with one accord,
All eyes were turned to Abraham Davenport.
He rose, slow cleaving with his steady voice
The intolerable hush: " This well may be
The Day of Judgment which the world awaits;
But be it so or not, I only know
My present duty, and my Lord's command
To occupy till he come.   So at the post
Where he hath set me in his providence
I choose, for one, to meet him face to face, —
No faithless servant frightened from my task,
But ready when the Lord of the harvest calls;
And therefore, with all reverence I would say,
Let God do his work, we will see to ours.
Bring in the candles."   And they brought them in.

Then by the flaring lights the Speaker read,
Albeit with husky voice and shaking hands,
An act to amend an act to regulate
The shad and alewive fisheries.   Whereupon
Wisely and well spake Abraham Davenport,
Straight to the question, with no figures of speech

Save the ten Arab signs, yet not without
The shrewd, dry humor natural to the man,
His awe-struck colleagues listening all the while,
Between the pauses of his argument,
To hear the thunder of the wrath of God
Break from the hollow trumpet of the cloud.

And there he stands in memory to this day,
Erect, self-poised, a rugged face half seen
Against the background of unnatural dark,
A witness to the ages as they pass
That simple duty hath no place for fear.

JOHN GREENLEAF WHITTIER.

YOUNG WINDEBANK.

THEY shot young Windebank just here,
By Merton, where the sun
Strikes on the wall.   'T was in a year
Of blood the deed was done.

At morning from the meadows dim
He watched them dig his grave.
Was this in truth the end for him,
The well-beloved and brave?

He marched with soldier scarf and sword,
Set free to die that day,
And free to speak once more the word
That marshalled men obey.

But silent on the silent band
    That faced him, stern as death,
He looked, and on the summer land,
    And on the grave beneath.

Then with a sudden smile and proud
    He waved his plume, and cried,
" The king! the king!" and laughed aloud,
    "The king! the king!" and died.

Let none affirm he vainly fell,
    And paid the barren cost
Of having loved and served too well
    A poor cause and a lost.

He in the soul's eternal cause
    Went forth as martyrs must, —
The kings who make the spirit laws,
    And rule us from the dust;

Whose wills, unshaken by the breath
    Of adverse Fate, endure
To give us honor strong as death,
    And loyal love as sure.

HERBERT P. HORNE.

PROSPICE.

FEAR death? — to feel the fog in my throat,
    The mist in my face,
When the snows begin, and the blasts denote
    I am nearing the place,

The power of the night, the press of the storm,
 The post of the foe;
Where he stands, the Arch Fear in a visible form,
 Yet the strong man must go·
For the journey is done and the summit attained,
 And the barriers fall,
Though a battle 's to fight ere the guerdon be gained,
 The reward of it all.
I was ever a fighter, so — one fight more,
 The best and the last!
I would hate that death bandaged my eyes, and forbore,
 And bade me creep past.
No! let me taste the whole of it, fare like my peers
 The heroes of old,
Bear the brunt, in a minute pay glad life's arrears
 Of pain, darkness, and cold.
For sudden the worst turns the best to the brave,
 The black minute 's at end,
And the elements' rage, the fiend voices that rave,
 Shall dwindle, shall blend,
Shall change, shall become first a peace, then a joy,
 Then a light, then thy breast,
O thou soul of my soul! I shall clasp thee again,
 And with God be the rest.

      ROBERT BROWNING.

AN ANGEL IN THE HOUSE.

HOW sweet it were if, without feeble fright,
Or dying of the dreadful, beauteous sight,
An angel came to us, and we could bear
To see him issue from the silent air
At evening in our room, and bend on ours
His divine eyes, and bring us from his bowers
News of dear friends, and children who have never
Been dead indeed, — as we shall know forever!
Alas! we think not what we daily see
About our hearths, angels that are to be,
Or may be if they will, and we prepare
Their souls and ours to meet in happy air, —
A child, a friend, a wife, whose soft heart sings
In unison with ours, breeding its future wings.

LEIGH HUNT.

WITH WHOM IS NO VARIABLENESS.

IT fortifies my soul to know
That, though I perish, Truth is so;
That, howsoe'er I stray and range,
Whate'er I do, Thou dost not change.
I steadier step when I recall
That, if I slip, Thou dost not fall.

ARTHUR HUGH CLOUGH.

LIFE IN OURSELVES.

DEAR artists, ye
— Whether in forms of curve or hue
Or tone your gospels be —
Say wrong, *This work is not of me,*
But God.   It is not true; it is not true.

Awful is Art, because 't is free.
The artist trembles o'er his plan,
Where men his Self must see.
Who made a song or picture, he
Did it, and not another, God nor man.

My Lord is large, my Lord is strong:
Giving, he gave; my Me is mine.
How poor, how strange, how wrong,
To dream he wrote the little song
I made to him with love's unforced design!

Pass, kinsman cloud, now fair and mild;
Discharge the will that 's not thine own.
I work in freedom wild,
But work, as plays a little child,
Sure of the Father, Self, and Love, alone.

SIDNEY LANIER.

INTEGER VITAE.

THE man of life upright,
　　Whose guiltless heart is free
From all dishonest deeds,
　　Or thoughts of vanity;

The man whose silent days
　　In harmless joys are spent,
Whom hopes cannot delude,
　　Nor sorrows discontent, —

That man needs neither towers
　　Nor armor for defence,
Nor secret vaults to fly
　　From thunder's violence.

He only can behold
　　With unaffrighted eyes
The horrors of the deep
　　And terrors of the skies.

Thus, scorning all the cares
　　That fate or fortune brings,
He makes the heaven his book,
　　His wisdom heavenly things,

Good thoughts his only friends,
　　His wealth a well-spent age,
The earth his sober inn
　　And quiet pilgrimage.

LORD BACON (?).

THE FIRE OF LIFE.

I STROVE with none, for none was worth my strife;
  Nature I loved, and next to Nature, Art;
I warmed both hands before the fire of life;
  It sinks, and I am ready to depart.

WALTER SAVAGE LANDOR.

NO COWARD SOUL.

NO coward soul is mine,
    No trembler in the world's storm-troubled
        sphere;
  I see heaven's glories shine,
And faith shines equal, arming me from fear.

  O God within my breast,
Almighty, ever-present Deity!
  Life that in me has rest,
As I, undying Life, have power in thee!

  Vain are the thousand creeds
That move men's hearts, unutterably vain;
  Worthless as withered weeds,
Or idlest froth amid the boundless main,

  To waken doubt in one
Holding so fast by thine infinity,
  So surely anchored on
The steadfast rock of immortality.

With wide-embracing love
The Spirit animates eternal years,
Pervades and broods above,
Changes, sustains, dissolves, creates, and rears.

Though earth and man were gone,
And suns and universes ceased to be,
And thou wert left alone,
Every existence would exist in thee.

There is not room for Death,
Nor atom that his might could render void:
Thou — thou art Being and Breath,
And what thou art may never be destroyed.

EMILY BRONTÉ.

THE DIVINE IMAGE.

TO mercy, pity, peace, and love,
    All pray in their distress,
And to these virtues of delight
    Return their thankfulness.

For mercy, pity, peace, and love,
    Is God, our Father dear;
And mercy, pity, peace, and love,
    Is man, His child and care.

For Mercy has a human heart;
    Pity, a human face;
And Love, the human form divine;
    And Peace, the human dress.

Then every man, of every clime,
   That prays in his distress,
Prays to the human form divine, —
   Love, Mercy, Pity, Peace.

And all must love the human form,
   In heathen, Turk, or Jew;
Where mercy, love, and pity dwell,
   There God is dwelling too.

WILLIAM BLAKE.

MY PRAYER.

GREAT God, I ask thee for no meaner pelf
   Than that I may not disappoint myself;
That in my action I may soar as high
As I can now discern with this clear eye;

And next in value that thy kindness lends,
That I may greatly disappoint my friends, —
Howe'er they think or hope that it may be,
They may not dream how thou 'st distinguished me;

That my weak hand may equal my firm faith,
And my life practise more than my tongue saith;
That my low conduct may not show,
   Nor my relenting lines,
That I thy purpose did not know,
   Or overrated thy designs.

HENRY D. THOREAU.

SOLEMN BEFORE US.

Translated from Goethe.

SOLEMN before us
   Looms the dark portal,
Goal of all mortal;
Stars silent rest over us;
Graves under us — silent.

But heard are the voices,
Heard are the sages,
The worlds and the ages:
Choose well; your choice is
Brief and yet endless.

Here eyes do regard you
In Eternity's stillness;
Here is all fulness,
Ye brave, to reward you:
Work, and despair not.

THOMAS CARLYLE.

THE STIRRUP-CUP.

DEATH, thou 'rt a cordial old and rare;
   Look how compounded, with what care!
Time got his wrinkles reaping thee
Sweet herbs from all antiquity.

David to thy distillage went,
Keats and Gotama excellent,
Omar Khayyám, and Chaucer bright,
And Shakspere for a king-delight.

Then, Time, let not a drop be spilt:
Hand me the cup whene'er thou wilt.
'T is thy rich stirrup-cup to me;
I 'll drink it down right smilingly.

SIDNEY LANIER.

HOPE EVERMORE AND BELIEVE.

From "*Amours de Voyage.*"

HOPE evermore and believe, O man; for e'en as
    thy thought,
  So are the things that thou seest, e'en as thy hope
    and belief.
Cowardly art thou, and timid? They rise to provoke
    thee against them.
  Hast thou courage? Enough!— see them exulting
    to yield.

Go from the east to the west, as the sun and the stars
    direct thee;
  Go with the girdle of man, go and encompass the
    earth.
Not for the gain of the gold, for the getting, the
    hoarding, the having;
  But for the joy of the deed, but for the Duty to do.

"HOPE EVERMORE."

From the painting, "Hope," by C. von Bodenhausen.

Go with the spiritual life, the higher volition and
    action ;
  With the great girdle of God go and encompass the
    earth.

Go with the sun and the stars, and yet evermore in thy
    spirit
  Say to thyself : It is good ; yet is there better than it.
This that I see is not all, and this that I do is but little ;
  Nevertheless it is good, though there is better than it.

ARTHUR HUGH CLOUGH.

TWO THOUGHTS.

WHEN I reflect how small a place I fill
    In this great, teeming world of laborers,
How little I can do with strongest will,
How marred that little by most hateful blurs, —
The fancy overwhelms me, and deters
My soul from putting forth so poor a skill :
Let me be counted with those worshippers
Who lie before God's altar and are still.
But then I think (for healthier moments come),
This power of will, this natural force of hand, —
What do they mean, if working be not wise ?
Forbear to weigh thy words, O Soul ! Arise,
And join thee to that nobler, sturdier band
Whose worship is not idle, fruitless, dumb.

EDWARD CRACROFT LEFROY.

THE SERVICE OF BEAUTY.

L ARGESS from sevenfold heavens, I pray, descend
    On all who toil for Beauty!   Never feet
Grow weary that have done her bidding sweet
About the careless world.   For she is friend
And darling of the universe; and day by day
She comes and goes, but never dies,
So precious is she in the eternal eyes.
Oh, dost thou scorn her, seeing what fine way
She doth avenge?   For heaven because of her
Shall one day find thee fitter.   How old hours
Of star-rapt night about thy heart had curled,
And thou hadst felt the morning's golden stir,
And the appealing loveliness of flowers, —
Yea, all the saving beauty of the world!

ANNE WHITNEY.

REMEMBER.

R EMEMBER me when I am gone away,
    Gone far away into the silent land,
When you can no more hold me by the hand,
Nor I half turn to go, yet, turning, stay.
Remember me when no more, day by day,
You tell me of our future that you planned.
Only remember me; you understand
It will be late to counsel then, or pray.

Yet, if you should forget me for a while
And afterwards remember, do not grieve;
For if the darkness and corruption leave
A vestige of the thoughts that once I had,
Better by far you should forget and smile,
Than that you should remember and be sad.

CHRISTINA GEORGINA ROSSETTI.

THE GOLDEN STRING.

I GIVE you the end of a golden string:
   Only wind it into a ball,
It will lead you in at Heaven's gate,
   Built in Jerusalem's wall.

WILLIAM BLAKE.

OPTIMISM.

WELL, and how good is life!
   Good to be born, have breath,
The calms good, and the strife,
   Good life, and perfect death.

EDWARD DOWDEN.

AH, YET CONSIDER IT AGAIN!

OLD things need not be therefore true,
   O brother men, nor yet the new.
Ah, still a while the old thought retain,
And yet consider it again!

The souls of now two thousand years
Have laid up here their toils and fears,
And all the earnings of their pain, —
Ah, yet consider it again!

We! what do *we* see?   Each a space
Of some few yards before his face.
Does that the whole wide plan explain?
Ah, yet consider it again!

Alas! the great world goes its way,
And takes the truth from each new day;
They do not quit, nor can retain,
Far less consider it again.

ARTHUR HUGH CLOUGH.

HIS BANNER OVER ME.

SURROUNDED by unnumbered foes,
    Against my soul the battle goes;
Yet, though I weary, sore distrest,
I know that I shall reach my rest.
  I lift my tearful eyes above;
  His banner over me is love.

Its sword my spirit will not yield,
Though flesh may faint upon the field;
He waves before my fading sight
The branch of palm, the crown of light.
  I lift my brightening eyes above;
  His banner over me is love.

My cloud of battle-dust may dim,
His veil of splendor curtain Him,
And in the midnight of my fear
I may not feel Him standing near;
  But, as I lift mine eyes above,
  His banner over me is love.

GERALD MASSEY.

ON, ON, FOREVER!

BENEATH this starry arch
  Nought resteth or is still;
But all things hold their march,
  As if by one great will.
Moves one, move all, — hark to the footfall!
  On, on, forever!

Yon sheaves were once but seed;
Will ripens into deed;
As cave-drops swell the streams,
Day-thoughts feed nightly dreams;
And sorrow tracketh wrong,
As echo follows song, —
  On, on, forever!

By night, like stars on high,
  The Hours reveal their train;
They whisper and go by:
  I never watch in vain.
Moves one, move all, — hark to the footfall!
  On, on, forever!

They pass the cradle-head,
And there a promise shed;
They pass the moist new grave,
And bid rank verdure wave;
They bear through every clime
The harvests of all time.
       On, on, forever!

          Harriet Martineau.

POTTER'S CLAY.

THOUGH the pitcher that goes to the sparkling rill
    Too often gets broken at last,
There are scores of others its place to fill
    When its earth to the earth is cast.
Keep that pitcher at home, let it never roam,
    But lie like a useless clod,
Yet sooner or later the hour will come
    When its chips are thrown to the sod.

Is it wise, then, say, in the waning day,
    When the vessel is cracked and old,
To cherish the battered potter's clay
    As though it were virgin gold?
Take care of yourself, dull, boorish elf, —
    Though prudent and safe you seem,
Your pitcher will break on the musty shelf,
    And mine by the dazzling stream.

          A. Lindsay Gordon.

THE CRICKET.

YES, the world is big, but I 'll do my best,
    Since I happen to find myself in it,
And I 'll sing my loudest out with the rest,
Though I 'm neither a lark nor a linnet,
And strive towards the goal with as tireless zest
Though I know I may never win it.

For shall no bird sing but the nightingale?
No flower bloom but the rose?
Shall lesser stars quench their torches pale
When Mars through the midnight glows?
Shall only the highest and greatest prevail?
May nothing seem white but the snows?

Nay, the world is so big that it needs us all
To make audible music in it.
God fits a melody e'en to the small;
We have nothing to do but begin it.
So I 'll chirp my merriest out with them all,
Though I 'm neither a lark nor a linnet.

GRACE DENIO LITCHFIELD.

THE HIDDEN LIFE.

WITHIN my life another life runs deep,
    To which, at blessed seasons, open wide
Silent, mysterious portals. There reside
These shapes that cautiously about me creep,
This iron mask of birth, and death, and sleep,
Familiar as the day and open-eyed;

And there broods endless calm.   And though it glide
Ofttimes beyond my sight, and though I keep
Its voice no more, I know the current flows
Pulsing to far-off harmonies, and light
With most unearthly heavens.   The world but throws
A passing spell thereon, as winter bright,
Pale feudatory of the arctic night,
Swathes with white silence all these murmurous
            boughs.
                              ANNE WHITNEY.

THE DEEPER THOUGHT.

BELOW the surface stream, shallow and light,
    Of what we *say* we feel, — below the stream,
As light, of what we *think* we feel, — there flows
With noiseless current, strong, obscure, and deep,
The central stream of what we feel indeed.
                              MATTHEW ARNOLD

THE APOLOGY.

THINK me not unkind and rude
    That I walk alone in grove and glen;
I go to the god of the wood
    To fetch his word to men.

Tax not my sloth that I
    Fold my arms beside the brook;
Each cloud that floated in the sky
    Writes a letter in my book.

Chide me not, laborious band,
　　For the idle flowers I brought;
Every aster in my hand
　　Goes home loaded with a thought.

There was never mystery
　　But 't is figured in the flowers,
Was never secret history
　　But birds tell it in the bowers.

One harvest from thy field
　　Homeward brought the oxen strong;
A second crop thine acres yield,
　　Which I gather in a song.

RALPH WALDO EMERSON.

WHO KNOWS?

From "Amours de Voyage."

SHALL we come out of it all some day, as one does
　　　　from a tunnel?
Will it be all at once, without our doing or asking,
We shall behold clear day, the trees and meadows
　　　　about us,
And the faces of friends, and the eyes we loved
　　　　looking at us?
Who knows? Who can say? It will not do to
　　　　suppose it.

ARTHUR HUGH CLOUGH.

THE TRAIL OF THE BUGLES.

IN early fall,
    When the world is still,
There comes a call
By river and hill, —

A breath of the passion
Of wilding land,
No lips can fashion,
No heart withstand.

The scarlet cry
Of a bugle's wail
Goes fading by
On a lonely trail;

And the heart of the year
Is braced and set
In battle gear
For the ages yet.

Once through the arch
Of the autumn wood
I saw the march
Of a giant brood.

I heard no tread
Of the warriors there,
But the hills were red
With the bugles' blare.

On the shadowy quest
That is never done
They strode abreast
Of the wheeling sun.

With no retreat,
Through the hazy flume
They marched to beat
At the gates of doom;

For these were they
Whom glory sealed
In the brunt of the fray
On sombre field.

By a goblin road,
Where the crimson line
Of maples glowed
In the deep blue pine,

Throng upon throng
They gathered and grew;
And all day long
On the hills they blew.

And ever I dream
Of a host since then,
And the moving gleam
Of marching men.

My heart is hot
With the bugles' cry;
And, tiring not,
Though the world go by,

Possessed and wild,
I must on and on
Like a marching child
With the warriors wan.

BLISS CARMAN.

WHAT MIGHT BE DONE.

WHAT might be done, if men were wise,
    What glorious deeds, my suffering brother,
        Would they unite
        In love and right,
And cease their scorn of one another?

Oppression's heart might be imbued
    With kindling drops of loving-kindness,
        And knowledge pour,
        From shore to shore,
Light on the eyes of mental blindness.

All slavery, warfare, lies, and wrongs,
    All vice and crime might die together;
        And wine and corn,
        To each man born,
Be free as warmth in summer weather.

The meanest wretch that ever trod,
    The deepest sunk in guilt and sorrow,
        Might stand erect
        In self-respect,
And share the teeming world to-morrow.

What might be done?   This might be done,
　And more than this, my suffering brother, —
　　More than the tongue
　　E'er said or sung,
If men were wise and loved each other.

CHARLES MACKAY

FLOWERS WITHOUT FRUIT.

PRUNE thou thy words, the thoughts control
　That o'er thee swell and throng;
They will condense within thy soul,
　And change to purpose strong.

But he who lets his feelings run
　In soft, luxurious flow,
Shrinks when hard service must be done,
　And faints at every woe.

Faith's meanest deed more favor bears,
　Where hearts and wills are weighed,
Than brightest transports, choicest prayers,
　Which bloom their hour and fade.

JOHN HENRY NEWMAN.

JESUS THE CARPENTER.

IS N'T this Joseph's son? Ay, it is he;
  Joseph, the carpenter, — same trade as me.
I thought as I 'd find it, — I knew it was here, —
    But my sight 's getting queer.

I don't know right where as his shed must ha' stood;
But often, as I 've been a-planing my wood,
I 've took off my hat just with thinking of he
    At the same work as me.

He warn't that set up that he could n't stoop down
And work in the country for folks in the town;
And I 'll warrant he felt a bit pride, like I 've done,
    At a good job begun.

The parson he knows that I 'll not make too free;
But on Sunday I feels as pleased as can be
When I wears my clean smock, and sits in a pew,
    And has thoughts not a few.

I think of as how not the parson hissen,
As is teacher and father and shepherd o' men, —
Not he knows as much of the Lord in that shed
    Where he earned his own bread.

And when I goes home to my missus, says she,
" Are you wanting your key? "
For she knows my queer ways and my love for the
      shed
    (We 've been forty years wed).

AT JOSEPH'S BENCH.

From the painting, "The Infancy of Christ," by H. Hoffmann.

So I comes right away by myself with the Book,
And I turns the old pages, and has a good look
For the text as I 've found as tells me as he
    Were the same trade as me.

Why don't I mark it?　Ah, many says so.
But I think I 'd as lief, with your leave, let it go ;
It do seem that nice when I fall on it sudden, —
    Unexpected, y' know.

CATHERINE C. LIDDELL

AT JOSEPH'S BENCH.

O LORD! at Joseph's humble bench
    Thy hands did handle saw and plane,
Thy hammer nails did drive and clench,
    Avoiding knot, and humoring grain.

That thou didst seem thou wast indeed ;
    In sport thy tools thou didst not use,
Nor, helping hind's nor fisher's need,
    The laborer's hire, too nice, refuse.

Lord, might I be but as a saw,
    A plane, a chisel, in thy hand!
No, Lord! I take it back in awe ;
    Such prayer for me is far too grand.

12

I pray, O Master! let me lie
　As on thy bench the favored wood;
Thy saw, thy plane, thy chisel ply,
　And work me into something good.

No, no; ambition, holy-high,
　Urges for more than both to pray:
Come in, O gracious Force! I cry;
　O Workman, share my shed of clay!

Then I, at bench, or desk, or oar,
　With last or needle, net or pen,
As thou in Nazareth of yore,
　Shall do the Father's will again.

GEORGE MACDONALD.

A PRAYER.

MAKER of the human heart,
　Scorn not thou thine own creation;
Onward guide its nobler part,
　Train it for its high vocation;
From the long-infected grain
Cleanse and purge each sinful stain;
Kindle with a kindred fire
Every good and great desire.

When in ruin and in gloom
　Falls to dust our earthly mansion,
Give us ample verge and room
　For the measureless expansion;

Clear our clouded mental sight
To endure thy piercing light;
Open wide our narrow thought
To embrace thee as we ought.

When the shadows melt away,
    And the eternal day is breaking,
Judge most just, be thou our stay
    In that strange and solemn waking.
Thou to whom the heart sincere
Is thy best of temples here,
May thy faithfulness and love
Be our long, last home above.

ARTHUR PENRHYN STANLEY.

THE WILL.

BLAME not the times in which we live,
    Nor Fortune, frail and fugitive;
Blame not thy parents, nor the rule
Of vice or wrong once learned at school;
    But blame thyself, O man!

Although both heaven and earth combined
To mould thy flesh and form thy mind;
Though every thought, word, action, will,
Was framed by powers beyond thee, — still
    Thou art thyself, O man!

And self to take or leave is free,
Feeling its own sufficiency;
In spite of science, spite of fate,
The judge within thee soon or late
    Will blame but thee, O man!

Say not, "I would, but could not. He
Should bear the blame who fashioned me.
Call you mere change of motive choice?"
Scorning such pleas, the inner voice
    Cries, "Thine the deed, O man!"

              JOHN ADDINGTON SYMONDS.

OPPOSITION.

OF fret, of dark, of thorn, of chill,
    Complain no more; for these, O heart,
Direct the random of thy will
    As rhymes direct the rage of art.

The lute's fixt fret, that runs athwart
    The strain and purpose of the string,
For governance and nice consort
    Doth bar his wilful wavering.

The dark hath many dear avails;
    The dark distils divinest dews;
The dark is rich with nightingales,
    With dreams, and with the heavenly Muse.

Bleeding with thorns of petty strife,
 I 'll ease (as lovers do) my smart
With sonnets to my lady Life,
 Writ red in issues from the heart.

What grace may lie within the chill
 Of favor frozen fast in scorn!
When Good 's a-freeze, we call it Ill;
 This rosy time is glacier-born.

Of fret, of dark, of thorn, of chill,
 Complain thou not, O heart; for these
Bank in the current of the will
 To uses, arts, and charities.

SIDNEY LANIER.

COURAGE.

HAST thou made shipwreck of thy happiness?
 Yet, if God please,
Thou 'lt find thee some small haven, none the less,
 In nearer seas,
Where thou mayst sleep for utter weariness,
 If not for ease.

The port thou dream'dst of thou shalt never reach,
 Though gold its gates,
And wide and fair the silver of its beach;
 For sorrow waits
To pilot all whose arms too far outreach,
 Toward darker straits.

Yet so no soul divine thou art astray;
    On this cliff's crown
Plant thou a victor flag ere breaks the day
    Across night's brown,
And none shall guess it doth but point the way
    Where a bark went down.

GRACE DENIO LITCHFIELD.

THROUGH LIFE.

WE slight the gifts that every season bears,
    And let them fall unheeded from our grasp,
    In our great eagerness to reach and clasp
The promised treasure of the coming years.

Or else we mourn some great good passed away,
    And, in the shadow of our grief shut in,
    Refuse the lesser good we yet might win,
The offered peace and gladness of to-day.

So through the chambers of our life we pass,
    And leave them, one by one, and never stay, —
Not knowing how much pleasantness there was
In each until the closing of the door
    Has sounded through the house, and died away,
And in our hearts we sigh, " Forevermore."

CHAMBERS'S JOURNAL.

THE CITY IN SPRING.

IT is not much that makes me glad:
   I hold more than I ever had;
The empty hand may farther reach,
And small, sweet signs all beauty teach.

I like the city in the spring;
It has a hint of everything.
Down in the yard I like to see
The budding of that single tree,

The little sparrows on the shed,
The scrap of soft sky overhead,
The cat upon the sunny wall, —
There's so much *meant* among them all.

The dandelion in the cleft
A broken pavement may have left,
Is like a star that, still and sweet,
Shines where the housetops almost meet.

I like a little; all the rest
Is somewhere, and the Lord knows best
How the whole robe hath grace for them
Who only touch the garment's hem.

ADELINE D. T. WHITNEY

A RECOMPENSE.

DEEPER my grief than I can say!
　　A thought is with me all the day, —
A thought that will not go away, —

That if my watchful care had been
More tender, and had hedged him in
The golden bars of Love between,

The Stranger, on his silent way,
The Stranger in the garments gray,
Had passed my darling by that day, —

Had spared the little life.　And yet,
If all to future moan and fret
The current of his days had set,

Could I be thankful?　Nay, not so;
Better the tentlet green and low,
Sweeter this truth that now I know.

I would not give so sweet a thing,
The shadow of my baby's wing,
For all the purples of a king.

I would not give the shining grace
That lingered on his fair, wee face,
For all the gifts of pride or place;

The memory of his joyous weeks
For all the bliss a lover seeks,
For all the lore a scholar speaks.

So go your way; I am content,
Remembering him without lament
For the brief space that he was lent.

MRS. D. H. CLARK.

IS IT SO SMALL A THING?

IS it so small a thing
    To have enjoyed the sun,
To have lived light in the spring,
To have loved, to have thought, to have done,
To have advanced true friends and beat down baffling
            foes,
That we must feign a bliss
Of doubtful future date,
And, while we dream on this,
Lose all our present state,
And delegate to worlds yet distant our repose?

MATTHEW ARNOLD.

DOWN THE DARK FUTURE.

LONG do the eyes that look from heaven see
    Time smoke, as in the spring the mulberry-tree,
With buds of battles opening fitfully,
Till Yorktown's winking vapors slowly fade,
And Time's full top casts down a pleasant shade
Where Freedom lies unarmed and unafraid.

SIDNEY LANIER.

THE TWO WAITINGS.

I.

DEAR hearts, you were waiting a year ago
    For the glory to be revealed;
You were wondering deeply, with bated breath,
    What treasure the days concealed.

Oh, would it be this, or would it be that?
    Would it be girl or boy?
Would it look like father or mother most?
    And what should you do for joy?

And then one day, when the time was full,
    And the spring was coming fast,
The tender grace of a life out-bloomed,
    And you saw your baby at last.

Was it or not what you had dreamed?
    It was, and yet it was not;
But, oh, it was better a thousand times
    Than ever you wished or thought!

II.

And now, dear hearts, you are waiting again,
    While the spring is coming fast;
For the baby that was a future dream
    Is now a dream of the past, —

A dream of sunshine and all that 's sweet,
   Of all that is pure and bright;
Of eyes that were blue as the sky by day,
   And as soft as the stars by night.

You are waiting again for the fulness of time,
   And the glory to be revealed;
You are wondering deeply, with aching hearts,
   What treasure is now concealed.

Oh, will she be this, or will she be that?
   And what will there be in her face
That will tell you sure that she is your own
   When you meet in the heavenly place?

As it was before, it will be again:
   Fashion your dream as you will;
When the veil is rent, and the glory is seen,
   It will more than your hope fulfil.

JOHN WHITE CHADWICK.

THOUGH ALL GREAT DEEDS.

THOUGH all great deeds were proved but fables
      fine;
  Though earth's old story could be told anew;
  Though the sweet fashions loved of them that sue
Were empty as the ruined Delphian shrine;

Though God did never man, in words benign,
  With sense of his great Fatherhood endue;
  Though life immortal were a dream untrue,
And he that promised it were not divine;
Though soul, though spirit were not, and all hope
  Reaching beyond the bourne melted away;
Though virtue had no goal and good no scope,
  But both were doomed to end with this, our day;
Though all these were not, to the ungraced heir
Would this remain, — to live as though they were.

JEAN INGELOW.

SOMEWHERE, SURELY.

From " In Rugby Chapel."

O STRONG soul, by what shore
    Tarriest thou now?   For that force,
Surely, has not been left vain!
Somewhere, surely, afar,
In the sounding labor-house vast
Of being, is practised that strength,
Zealous, beneficent, firm!

Yes, in some far-shining sphere,
Conscious or not of the past,
Still thou performest the word
Of the spirit in whom thou dost live,
Prompt, unwearied, as here.

Still thou upraisest with zeal
The humble good from the ground,
Sternly repressest the bad;
Still, like a trumpet, dost rouse
Those who with half-open eyes
Tread the borderland dim
'Twixt vice and virtue, reviv'st,
Succorest. This was thy work,
This was thy life upon earth.

And through thee I believe
In the noble and great who are gone;
Pure souls, honored and blest
By former ages, who else —
Such, so soul-less, so poor,
Is the race of men whom I see —
Seemed but a dream of the heart,
Seemed but a cry of desire.
Yes, I believe that there lived
Others like thee in the past,
Not like the men of the crowd
Who all round me to-day
Bluster or cringe, and make life
Hideous, and arid, and vile;
But souls tempered with fire,
Fervent, heroic, and good,
Helpers and friends of mankind.

Servants of God! — or sons
Shall I not call you? because
Not as servants ye knew
Your Father's innermost mind,

His, who unwillingly sees
One of his little ones lost, —
Yours is the praise if mankind
Hath not as yet in its march
Fainted, and fallen, and died.

See! in the rocks of the world
Marches the host of mankind,
A feeble, wavering line.
Where are they tending? A God
Marshalled them, gave them their goal.
Ah, but the way is so long!
Years they have been in the wild!
Sore thirst plagues them; the rocks,
Rising all round, overawe;
Factions divide them; their host
Threatens to break, to dissolve.
Ah, keep, keep them combined!
Else, of the myriads who fill
That army, not one shall arrive;
Sole they shall stray; on the rocks
Batter forever in vain,
Die one by one in the waste.

Then in such hour of need
Of your failing, dispirited race,
Ye, like angels, appear;
Radiant with ardor divine,
Beacons of hope, ye appear.
Languor is not in your heart,
Weakness is not in your word,
Weariness not on your brow.

FOUNDLING GIRLS.

From the painting by Mrs. Anderson.

Ye alight in our van! At your voice,
Panic, despair, flee away.
Ye move through the ranks, recall
The stragglers, refresh the outworn,
Praise, reinspire the brave.
Order, courage, return;
Eyes rekindling, and prayers,
Follow your steps as ye go.
Ye fill up the gaps in our files,
Strengthen the wavering line,
Stablish, continue our march,
On to the bounds of the waste,
On to the City of God.

MATTHEW ARNOLD.

LIFE AND SONG.

IF life were caught by a clarionet,
 And a wild heart, throbbing in the reed,
Should thrill its joy and trill its fret,
 And utter its heart in every deed,

Then would this breathing clarionet
 Type what the poet fain would be
For none of the singers ever yet
 Has wholly lived his minstrelsy,

Or clearly sung his true, true thought,
 Or utterly bodied forth his life,
Or out of life and song has wrought
 The perfect one of man and wife,

Or lived and sung, that Life and Song
  Might each express the other's all,
Careless if life or art were long,
  Since both were one, to stand or fall:

So that the wonder struck the crowd,
  Who shouted it about the land:
His song was only living aloud,
  His work, a singing with his hand!

SIDNEY LANIER.

UNDER THE CLOUD.

O BEAUTEOUS things of earth!
  I cannot feel your worth
    To-day.

O kind and constant friend!
Our spirits cannot blend
    To-day.

O Lord of truth and grace!
I cannot see Thy face
    To-day.

A shadow on my heart
Keeps me from all apart
    To-day.

Yet something in me knows
How fair creation glows
    To-day.

And something makes me sure
That love is not less pure
　　To-day.

And that th' Eternal Good
Minds nothing of my mood
　　To-day.

For when the sun grows dark,
A sacred, secret spark
　　Shoots rays.

Fed from a hidden bowl,
A lamp burns in my soul
　　All days.
　　　　　CHARLES G. AMES.

LOVE.

TO love and seek return,
　　To ask but only this,
To feel where we have poured our heart
　　The spirit's answering kiss;
To dream that now our eyes
　　The brightening eyes shall meet,
And that the word we 've listened for
　　Our hungering ears shall greet, —
　　How human and how sweet!

To love nor find return,
　　Our hearts poured out in vain,
No brightening look, no answering tone,
　　Left lonely with our pain;

The opened heavens closed,
Night when we looked for morn,
The unfolding blossom harshly chilled,
Hope slain as soon as born, —
How bitter, how forlorn

To love nor ask return,
To accept our solitude;
Not now for others' love to yearn,
But only for their good;
To joy if they are crowned,
Though thorns our head entwine,
And in the thought of blessing them
All thought of self resign, —
How godlike, how divine!

SAMUEL LONGFELLOW.

SILENT PRAYER.

SELDOM upon lips of mine,
Father! rests that name of thine:
Deep within my inmost breast,
In the secret place of mind,
Doth the dread idea rest.
Hushed and holy dwells it there,
Prompter of the silent prayer,
Lifting up my spirit's eye,
And its faint but earnest cry
From its dark and cold abode,
Unto thee, my guide and God!

AFTER LAMARTINE.

LIFE.

FORENOON and afternoon and night, forenoon
And afternoon and night, forenoon and — what?
The empty song repeats itself.   No more?
Yea, this is Life: make this forenoon sublime,
This afternoon a psalm, this night a prayer,
And Time is conquered, and thy crown is won.

EDWARD ROWLAND SILL.

CROSSING THE BAR.

SUNSET and evening star,
And one clear call for me!
And may there be no moaning of the bar
When I put out to sea,

But such a tide as moving seems asleep,
Too full for sound and foam,
When that which drew from out the boundless deep
Turns again home.

Twilight and evening bell,
And after that the dark!
And may there be no sadness of farewell
When I embark;

For though from out our bourne of Time and Place
The flood may bear me far,
I hope to see my Pilot face to face
When I have crossed the bar.

ALFRED TENNYSON.

BEATI ILLI.

BLEST is the man whose heart and hands are pure!
He hath no sickness that he shall not cure,
No sorrow that he may not well endure;
His feet are steadfast, and his hope is sure.

Oh, blest is he who ne'er hath sold his soul;
Whose will is perfect, and whose word is whole;
Who hath not paid to common sense the toll
Of self-disgrace, nor owned the world's control!

Through clouds and shadows of the darkest night
He will not lose a glimmering of the light,
Nor, though the sun of day be shrouded quite,
Swerve from the narrow path to left or right.

JOHN ADDINGTON SYMONDS.

TO-DAY.

LO, here hath been dawning another blue day;
Think, wilt thou let it slip useless away?

Out of eternity this new day is born,
Into eternity at night will return.

Behold it aforetime no eye ever did;
So soon it forever from all eyes is hid.

Here hath been dawning another blue day;
Think, wilt thou let it slip useless away?

THOMAS CARLYLE.

ON LIFE'S ROUGH SEA.

GIVE me a spirit that on this life's rough sea
 Loves to have his sails filled with a lusty wind,
Even till his sail-yards tremble, his masts crack,
And his rapt ship runs on her side so low
That she drinks water, and her keel ploughs air.
There is no danger to a man that knows
What life and death is, — there's not any law
Exceeds his knowledge; neither is it lawful
That he should stoop to any other law.

GEORGE CHAPMAN.

FAREWELL.

THOU goest; to what distant place
 Wilt thou thy sunlight carry?
I stay with cold and clouded face;
 How long am I to tarry?
Where'er thou goest morn will be;
Thou leavest night and gloom to me.

The night and gloom I can but take;
 I do not grudge thy splendor;
Bid souls of eager men awake,
 Be kind and bright and tender.
Give day to other worlds; for me
It must suffice to dream of thee.

JOHN ADDINGTON SYMONDS.

EN VOYAGE.

WHICHEVER way the wind doth blow,
    Some heart is glad to have it so;
Then blow it east or blow it west,
The wind that blows, that wind is best.

My little craft sails not alone;
A thousand fleets from every zone
Are out upon a thousand seas;
And what for me were favoring breeze
Might dash another with the shock
Of doom upon some hidden rock.
And so I do not dare to pray
For winds to waft me on my way,
But leave it to a Higher Will
To stay or speed me, trusting still
That all is well, and sure that He
Who launched my bark will sail with me
Through storm and calm, and will not fail,
Whatever breezes may prevail,
To land me, every peril past,
Within his sheltering heaven at last.

Then, whatsoever wind doth blow,
My heart is glad to have it so;
And blow it east or blow it west,
The wind that blows, that wind is best.

CAROLINE A. MASON.

WAITING.

SERENE I fold my arms and wait,
  Nor care for wind, or tide, or sea;
I rave no more 'gainst time or fate,
  For, lo, my own shall come to me.

I stay my haste, I make delays;
  For what avails this eager pace?
I stand amid the eternal ways,
  And what is mine shall know my face.

Asleep, awake, by night or day,
  The friends I seek are seeking me;
No wind can drive my bark astray,
  Nor change the tide of destiny.

What matter if I stand alone?
  I wait with joy the coming years;
My heart shall reap where it has sown,
  And garner up its fruit of tears.

The waters know their own, and draw
  The brook that springs in yonder height;
So flows the good with equal law
  Unto the soul of pure delight.

The floweret nodding in the wind
  Is ready plighted to the bee;
And, maiden, why that look unkind?
  For, lo! thy lover seeketh thee.

The stars come nightly to the sky,
　　The tidal wave unto the sea;
Nor time, nor space, nor deep, nor high,
　　Can keep my own away from me.

JOHN BURROUGHS.

SAY NOT THE STRUGGLE NAUGHT AVAILETH.

SAY not the struggle naught availeth,
　　The labor and the wounds are vain,
The enemy faints not, nor faileth,
　　And as things have been they remain.

If hopes were dupes, fears may be liars;
　　It may be, in yon smoke concealed,
Your comrades chase e'en now the fliers,
　　And but for you possess the field.

For while the tired waves, vainly breaking,
　　Seem here no painful inch to gain,
Far back, through creeks and inlets making,
　　Comes silent flooding in the main.

And not by eastern windows only,
　　When daylight comes, comes in the light;
In front the sun climbs slow, how slowly !
　　But westward, look, the land is bright.

ARTHUR HUGH CLOUGH.

ANTI-DESPERATION.

LONG fed on boundless hopes, O race of man,
    How angrily thou spurn'st all simpler fare!
Christ, some one says, was human as we are;
No judge eyes us from heaven, our sin to scan;

We live no more when we have done our span.
"Well, then, for Christ," thou answerest, "who can
        care?
From sin which heaven records not, why forbear?
Live we like brutes, our life without a plan!"

So answerest thou; but why not rather say:
"Hath man no second life? Pitch this one high!
Sits there no judge in heaven our sin to see?

"More strictly, then, the inward judge obey!
Was Christ a man like us? Ah, let us try
If we, then, too, can be such men as he!"

                    MATTHEW ARNOLD

ONE GREAT DESIRE.

CLING to the flying hours, and yet
    Let one pure hope, one great desire,
Like song on dying lips be set, —
    That e'er we fall in scattered fire
    Our hearts may lift the world's heart higher.

Here in these autumn months of time,
    Before the great New Year shall break,
Some little way our feet should climb,
    Some little mark our hands should make,
    For liberty and manhood's sake.

EDMUND GOSSE

THE BOOK OF MARTYRS.

READ, sweet, how others strove,
    Till we are stouter;
What they renounced,
Till we are less afraid;
How many times they bore
The faithful witness,
Till we are helped
As if a kingdom cared.

Read then of faith
That shone above the fagot,
Clear strains of hymn
The river could not drown,
Brave names of men
And celestial women
Passed out of record
Into renown.

EMILY DICKINSON.

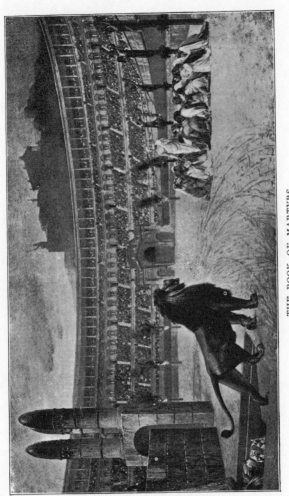

THE BOOK OF MARTYRS.

From the painting, " The Last Prayer," by Gerome.

THE WANDERER.

THE gleam of household sunshine ends,
   And here no longer can I rest.
Farewell! You will not speak, my friends,
Unkindly of your parted guest.

Oh, well for him that finds a friend,
Or makes a friend, where'er he come,
And loves the world from end to end,
And wanders on from home to home!

Oh, happy he, and fit to live,
On whom a happy home has power
To make him trust his life, and give
His fealty to the halcyon hour!

I count you kind, I hold you true;
But what may follow, who can tell?
Give me a hand — and you — and you —
And deem me grateful — and farewell!

                 ALFRED TENNYSON.

INDEX OF FIRST LINES.

———————♦———————